IT'S ALL IN THE WAY YOU LOOK AT THINGS

by

Dr. Cornell Thomas

Published by: CGS Communications
Fort Worth, Texas

It's All In The Way You Look At Things

CGS Communications
Publishing Company
Post Office Box 17485
Fort Worth, Texas 76102

First Printing November 1996

Library of Congress Catalog Card Number
96-071456

Cover design by Ascension Graphics

Printed in the United States of America.

DEDICATION

To Johnetta, My Wife

You are the pep in my step

My sunshine every day

The heat pump connected to my heart

You are the JOY in my life

I thank my LORD for answering prayers

Prayers making you and me—WE

You have let me experience the joys of life and the exquisite pleasures of your own eternal presence.

PSALMS 16:11

TABLE OF CONTENTS

ACKNOWLEDGMENTS

Inspiration is a magnificent phenomenon. Occurrence and recurring are truly a blessing. Because of the many inspirational blessings sent my way, this work exists. Blessings, all from GOD, have come in various shapes, sizes, colors and manners. I want to take this moment in time to recognize some of them with thanksgiving.

To my friends Jacqueline Diggles, LaRon Wilson, Clark Carter, Phyllis Bodie, Renee Gordon, Etta Miller, Mattie Compton and Lincoln Butler, your conversations have been invaluable. Doug Simpson and Mike Sacken have both provided a strong foundation, as mentors and friends, on which one can stand firm in this arena.

A special recognition to two individuals who are truly GOD's tools, Jerome and Billye McNeil—I love you both.

My beginnings and a continuing source of inspiration are traced back to Eugene and Marie Thomas, my parents and head of a family I hold most dear.

The circle, the constellation is complete with the addition of Ronjanett, Marsha and Goldie, my beautiful, loving, Christian daughters.

The process of continued transformation receives energy from the union of three, GOD, my wife Johnetta and me.

May GOD'S Blessings Continue.

AMEN

FOREWORD

Cornell Thomas, in *It's All In The Way You Look At Things*, describes how individuals are affected by previous experiences and other inputs from their immediate environment. He uses relevant cases and real-life experiences to describe how negative and positive interactions may enable individuals to build barriers or bridges, depending on the perspectives they have formed. He implies that it is difficult to achieve racial harmony and the ability to reach the American Dream due to disharmony created in our society.

The author expresses that we must create a new vision for society if we are to move into the 21st Century and become more productive and positive than in the past. Emphasis should be placed on the need to discover ways of affirming and utilizing the new diversity that is ours to build a common set of values. This, hopefully, will enable us to develop a sense of community that is needed to survive and improve society.

Dr. Thomas devotes considerable time to overcoming historic inequities and social stereotypes, rethinking what schools do, the role of leadership (principal, teacher), assimilation, and dreams deferred. Finally, he espouses a strong position concerning understanding the total, perceiving the negative from a positive and realistic/different perspective. Transformation and enlightment could result which will create a renaissance movement to positively affect the psychological, physical, and other aspects of African American life.

This manuscript is a must reading for principals, teachers, and others who are responsible for determining policies, curriculum and other operating procedures that impact the education of our youth. Any transformation or renaissance in society may be fueled by creating an understanding of diversity. And we must use this diversity as a strength to achieve a common mission to ensure equity and justice for individuals who are different (age, ethnic heritage, physical ability, religious beliefs, sexual orientation).

Alfred L. Roberts, Sr., Ph.D. Edc.
Executive Director, Alternative Certification
Dallas Public Schools
Past President
National Alliance of Black School Educators

1

BEGINNING

> Once upon a time, of course, many thought that racial division would soon be a thing of the past, that the next generation, or perhaps the one after that, would achieve harmony where their parents could not. Martin Luther King's may have been the most famous 1960s dream, but he was not dreaming alone. Yet as today's young people come of age, many one time idealists are beginning to think that such dreams are rooted in little more than fantasy (Cose, 1993, p.146).

Individuals often interpret their interactions with others based on previous experiences and other inputs from their immediate environment. For example, if an individual is born and raised in a racist environment, one in which family members speak of or do things considered to be racist, the likelihood is that the individual will model this form of behavior. These past experiences and inputs, both negative and positive, act as building blocks with which we can build barriers or bridges, depending on the perspective we formulate about our world. If we use our building blocks in a negative way, we impede the process of learning new points of view. The resulting mind-set makes it difficult for us to respect and value the opinions and actions of others.

Historically, African Americans have generally experienced a dominant Anglo population that regards them as less qualified and lacking the ability to assume equally responsible roles and avenues of opportunity, when compared to themselves, in this, our society. African Americans have been subjected to a wide range of theories regarding their physical, emotional and intellectual attributes, or lack thereof. Particularly, dominant Anglo societal leadership has propagated misconceptions devaluing the African American by using, among other techniques, out-of-context biblical quotations, questionable scientific research findings, erroneous data-gathering methods, ancient historical perspectives and cultural deprivation concepts. The very classification of ethnic groups into categories of race was fueled, in part, by a need to legitimize the treatment of a group of fellow human beings in such despicable, deplorable, un-Godly ways. Communication networks were and are vehicles that enhance the perpetuation of the premises left by these and other numerous attempts to create a subhuman human being. However, these same channels of communication are also being employed to present different and more positive perspectives.

Creating a new vision for society is critical if we are to travel into the twenty-first century in a more productive and positive way than in the past. There is a need, therefore, to find ways of prizing and utilizing the new diversity that exists and to unearth a common set of values that will facilitate the development of the concept of community most proclaim, at least publicly, is necessary for survival of our society. One would think or at least hope that history will not repeat itself in this instance. However, some seem to have lost hope.

This issue of diversity becomes a primary concern when leadership attempts to develop within an organization, a school for instance, a sense of community among diverse mind-sets. Simply to address theoretical, philosophical, and paradigmatic disagreements in schools is not enough. We must also concern ourselves with preferential, prudential, ethnic and other kinds of differences. These differences often center around the issue of race and thus become building blocks that form formidable barriers against the creation of any true concept of community within diverse settings. Therefore, since diversity best describes our current society and is seen by many of its members as possibly destructive if not addressed appropriately, the issue becomes one of major concern.

2

SELF-IMAGE: EXAMINING OUR PERSONAL HISTORY

> Who am I, then? Foremost, I am a child of God, created in his image, imbued with his spirit, endowed with his gifts, set free by his grace. The most important challenges and opportunities that confront me derive not from my racial condition, but rather from my human condition. I am a husband, a father, a son, a teacher, an intellectual, a Christian, a citizen. In none of these roles is my race irrelevant, but neither can racial identity alone provide much guidance for my quest to adequately discharge these responsibilities. The particular features of my social condition, the external givens, merely set the stage of my life, they do not provide a script. That script must be internally generated, it must be a product of a reflective deliberation about the meaning of this existence for which no political or ethnic program could ever substitute (Glenn C. Loury, 1993).

If history often repeats itself, then a study of the past will bring clarity to events in both the present and future. The same can be said of an individual's history. Past events play a critical role in present and future events, reactions, and decisions. Many are of the opinion that it is this "past" that makes up the foundation on which we live our lives. And it is the building of strong foundations that enhances the possibilities for a good, productive, and spiritually satisfying life.

For example, the development of each individual can be compared to how a composer creates a musical work of art. A composer might create a harmonious piano concerto with each chord progressing smoothly through predictable chord changes, ending with a feeling of total fulfillment. A composition might describe a love story, one full of happiness, then tragedy, and back to love everlasting, or an ending of despair and hate. The syncopated, agitated, often unorthodox rhythms of Rap might demonstrate the confusion, mistrust, and hate often seen in many of our youth of today. Or a spiritual full of uplifting, augmented chord changes can stimulate thoughts that although times are hard now, a brighter, better day is yet to come—hope. You see, each of the examples uses the same notes, but it is the combination of notes that makes up the resulting compositions.

> There were a number of white families on our block when we first arrived; within a couple of years they had all been replaced by aspiring black families like our own. I often wondered why Woody's parents never moved. Then I overheard his mother declare to one of her new neighbors, "We just wouldn't run from our own kind," a comment that befuddled me at the time. Somewhat later, while we were watching the movie *Imitation of Life* on television, my mother explained how someone could be black though he or she looked white. She told me about people like that in our own family—second cousins living in a fashionable suburb on whom one would never dare simply to drop in because they were "passing for white." This was my earliest glimpse of the truth that racial identity in America is inherently a social and cultural, not simply a biological construct—that it necessarily involves an irreducible element of choice (Loury, 1993, p. 2).

Our life experiences combine to form the harmonious or discordant themes of our existence, our sense of ourselves. Consider the early history of Amad and Kareem:

CASE IN POINT

Amad and Kareem are 17-year-old cousins whose immediate male role models are hard-working uncles who hate their factory jobs that require long hours of repetitive, boring work, jobs diminishing in pay and that today are even hard to come by. Because of recent massive business layoffs and corporate downsizing, John and Leslie see bleaker futures for themselves: a future of living paycheck to paycheck at best; a future with wives constantly wanting more and children needing more; a future controlled too much by the "MAN." Amad and Kareem look back at eleven years of education and begin to scrutinize the type of preparation they have been afforded. Both have begun to realize that they are not prepared for college, that technical training is being presented by their counselors and teachers as possibly their only viable option toward any type of professional career, and that the system has predetermined their standing in the social order. Amad and Kareem are good, respectful young men who are confused, angry and ready to aggressively respond to what they and many other young African American men feel has been society's systematic denial of equal access to the American Dream. Their uncles have tried to talk with them about the importance of education, and although their grades, all As and Bs, reflect their belief in and commitment to what they heard, recent PSAT scores demonstrate their lack of the educational experiences needed to be successful in their anticipated post-secondary pursuits.

Are these more dreams deferred? Why does our tiered educational system exist? A system that has different expectations and therefore different curricula for African American students. And why does this system have such negative effects on the poor, especially on African American males? What decisions will these and other young men in this situation make as they strive for a future of comfort and security? How can this cycle of despair be altered and by whom? Before answering these questions, further exploration of the problem is in order.

The way we conceptualize and function within varying environments is greatly influenced by our personal experiences. In our formative years, parents are the primary composers of our life themes. Others touch young lives in varying degrees. These early influences in our lives are successful when they build bridges, connecting what they want children to know with what they already know. They fail when their influence throws barriers in the path of true learning and self-development. Some of the major influences in the lives of the young today are peers, television, other adults, church and educators.

Negative subliminal messages can be seen and heard every day on television, on the radio, in movie theaters, and read in newspaper articles. It is amazing to realize that a seemingly harmless form of entertainment can be harmful, like popular television sitcoms in which people seem to occupy a universe devoid of ethnic diversity like "Cheers" or "Seinfeld." Some would argue that similarly negative types of messages can be seen depicting almost every ethnic and racial group in this society. However, positive depictions compensate or, in many cases, overcompensate for almost every group except for African Americans.

> If we looked only at the electronic and print media, we would believe that the majority of criminals, drug-users, prostitutes, drunks, illiterates, high school dropouts, juvenile delinquents, jobless, and poor people in this country were African Ameri-

> cans. The fact is that most of these are White, not African Americans. Nor would we know that the vast majority of African Americans are none of the above. Thus, powerful visions can neither be built on the paralysis of the present realities nor on the negative thoughts of influential people and institutions. Both of these are blinded by their limited paradigms and therefore cannot see the possibilities of our vision (Hamilton, 1990).

The narrowness of Eurocentric viewpoints in our society as they relate to African Americans, along with the high degree of racism that permeates the very core of this society, fuels a wall of fire. This barrier prevents the establishment of equal and positive growing relationships between Whites and African Americans, who make up a significant portion of our country. Individuals seeking a positive change must begin to clearly understand this concept of racism in order to find ways of diminishing its negative effects.

Negative images of ourselves and each other help shape attitudes and practices in our schools. The impact of negative images on the attitudes and opinions of our young African American children is tremendous. It is these negative images, often unspoken but no less in operation, that have helped to create an environment of extremely low expectations for the achievable levels of success by the majority of African American students.

These attitudes and beliefs also play a critical role in the development of teacher-student relationships in the classroom, the students' level of intrinsic motivation for learning, and the role of the parent in the teaching/learning process. Thus these attitudes become major factors in the success or failure of the child and eventually the entire social system.

And so it is these and other critical elements that bring us together in this book. A discussion of our children's most important influence, our educators, will be of primary concern as we explore the issues that young African Americans face.

A PRAYER FOR THE YOUNG ONES

> Why now, young Black men, have you decided to live in the present? What happened to the future vision of your grandfathers and great-grandfathers? Why now do you have to go to jail before you take time to commune with ourselves? Why do you have to be on death row before you decide to read a book or study law or heroically save someone's life? Your generation talks a lot about "roles." What "role" will you play in life? Try man. Try responsible man. Try forward-looking man. Try man who learns something the easy way (college) instead of the hard way (prison). Try doing the very difficult job of helping yourself and someone else by building something. Try honoring the very best in yourself instead of the very worst (Giovanni, 1994, p. 98).

Perhaps the devastating loss of life among our young African American population will soon end—it must. When looking at statistical analyses of the situation, or just sitting at home watching or reading the news, one is saddened by the lack of respect for fellow man. This lack of respect is often demonstrated by the enormous numbers of murders, robberies, assaults, unemployed, undereducated, and the disenfranchised in our society.

When the effects of such carnage touch family and other loved ones, when it is actually lived, only faith and hope keeps one from giving up. Some choose to fight back, often resulting in even more devastating circumstances. Fighting back is considered an effective tool for many individuals wanting change. The question then becomes what constitutes effective and productive "fighting?" How should we fight back? Is the fight really worth the effort or is tiered citizenship in this society as perceived by some, especially those at or near the bottom tiers, an unchangeable system in which the rich get richer and the poor, poorer? Cose (1993) brings focus to this concern.

> In some respects, the answer to "why are these people so angry?" Is not at all simple. For one thing, none are angry all the time. A few deny their anger even as they show it. And while all African Americans, in one way or another, have spent their lives coping with racial demons, the impact has not been identical. Some have been beaten into an almost numb submission, into accepting that they will never reach the goals they once thought possible. Others have refused to accept that being black means being treated as a lesser human being, and they respond to each insult with furious indignation. A number wonder whether, given the blessings they have received, they have any right to be angry at all (p.13).

What are the prospects for a newborn, healthy baby boy —African American. The chances for what we would like to consider a normal life for this newborn seem to diminish with each passing day. Yet, the prospects for many other healthy newborns, newborns not of color and/or considered less disadvantaged, are more positive. Consider the words of Michael Wynn:

> The African-American male is an endangered species. The 1990 U.S. Census Bureau figures show that African-American males have higher unemployment rates; lower labor force participation rates; lower high school graduation and college

> enrollment rates; while ranking first in incarceration and homicide as a percentage of the population. . . The leading cause of death for African-American men between the ages of 15 and 24 is homicide. And, while representing only 6 percent of the population, African-American men represent 49 percent of prison inmates. Only 4 percent of African-American males attend college, while 23 percent of those of college age are either incarcerated, on probation, or in prison. While African-American children nationwide comprise approximately 17 percent of all children in public schools, they represent 41 percent of all children in special education. Of the African-American children in special education, 85 percent of them are African-American males. African-American males, while comprising only 8 percent of public school students, represent the largest percentage, nationally, in suspensions (37 percent), (Wynn, 1992, p. xvii).

Why is there such a drastic variance in projected life-styles? Is awareness of the limitations in life choices a continuing source of civil unrest? And is this drastic variance in projected life-styles a major cause of the lack of respect for fellow man?

Leo Buscaglia once stated, "The future belongs to those of us who believe in the beauty of our dreams." What type of dreams does he mean? Dreams of living in a society based on the premise of equality of opportunity? A democratic society in which all are afforded the rights and privileges contained in our Constitution? A Constitution envisioning a society where there exists a high level of trust and respect among the citizenry? A society in which one's perspective is valued and included in decision-making processes? A community prospering from a collective mind-set where all citizens are granted the opportunity to share in the "American Dream?" An American Dream in which happiness, prosperity, peace and love are focal points. What happens when thoughts and experiences are regrettably focused upon sadness, poverty, negative aggression and hate? We see more and more children experiencing combinations of many of the negative aspects of life today, especially poor children and children of color, often one and the same. These children suffer to a much higher degree from the effects of a life filled with much uncertainty, violence, sadness, lack of structure, lack of love, lack of the positive experiences needed to enhance chances for the type of life we all desire—*lack of hope.* A life that clouds dreams with nightmares, imagined and lived. A life lacking beautiful dreams of the future. A life with little hope. One must pray for the young ones.

JAMES' STORY

I'm a man, but what does that really mean? I mean, well I graduated from high school last year and really have had only one brush with the law. I worked during my junior and senior years in high school but, where the money went. Hey, I don't know.

My uncle started, during my junior year, seriously asking me about college every time he came back home or caught me answering the phone when he called. You see he's worked hard and gotten a good education. I think he had a better chance when he was my age. Well anyway, he sent letters to different colleges for me and man! I really didn't know what I wanted to do. I remembered how my uncle gave me this book entitled *Visions For Black Men* by Na'im Akbar. The book, and discussions with my uncle, really made me understand the difference between being a *MALE* and being a *MAN*. I also realized that I did not as yet measure up to Akbar's definition of what it means to be a man, or mine for that matter. My uncle made sure my financial aid forms were completed and basically talked me into selecting and then going to a college.

Man, was college a *Different World* for me! From the very beginning I realized some of the things I had taken for granted. For example, I had to make sure I got up to go to class. I had to wash my own laundry and clean my room. And what really tripped me out was the fact that I now had to budget my money! These were responsibilities (along with others) I never had to deal with. My mother took care of these things back home. On top of this responsibility thing, I had to learn how to study. See, in high school my class work was not really much of a challenge. I mean I could and did do well without much study. My study habits, if you would be nice enough to call them study habits, would probably be comparable to that of an average sixth grader. Suffice it to say, my grades proved to be an accurate reflection of my poor study habits. Another problem that affected my grades was the drinking habit I developed before leaving home and which was now escalating in college. I drank to relieve the confusion, the pain, the sadness, and to sleep.

I understand, to some degree, the plight of the Black man in today's society. I know that the road is tough, full of extra steep hills, barriers, and a much more hazardous terrain than traveled by my white counterparts. I know that going home (quitting, which I constantly think about) will be a tremendous blow to my chances toward achieving some level of autonomy in life. But, sometimes I wonder if it is all worth it. I mean, even if I do finish school, will I have the same opportunities as my white male (or even female) counterparts? Will doors really open for me, providing opportunities to prove my abilities or will there be just a little crack in the door, letting only tokens in who happen to be in the right place at the right time?

I look back at my life and see the many negative things that have already occurred. I never really had a father. He died before I turned two years of age. [It was the system that drove him to his death—being murdered]. So I never really connected with an older male figure. There was never a sense of closeness/bonding felt, something I really needed. I had uncles and a grandfather, but they didn't take the step to help. It was as though they thought I was doing all right. Man, I lived with my mom and sisters! I had no concept or model of what it meant to be a responsible, strong Black Man. I often thought of talking with my youngest uncle, but he was in college, which seemed to consume all of his time. I eventually connected with a cousin who was like a big brother. He was somewhat alienated from the family because he was a hustler and later he became a gangbanger. Well, while at school, only into my second month, he was killed in a drive-by. Once again, a connection was severed! I do often wonder if it's [school] all worth it, I wonder.

I love my mom, but I see what she is doing with her life, *nothing*! I mean she did her best to raise us and make our lives happy. Actually, she did a good job. However, she failed to plan for the future. So she has no money coming in, since we have all graduated from high school, and no job. She and we now live with her mother and father. As I said, I love my mom but it is hard to find respect for her. There are other circumstances surrounding this feeling, but we don't need to expose all of that stuff. I am respectful to her, but I lack respect for her. All of these factors have had a tremendous influence on the quality of work (and thus grades) I made during my first semester in college. My grades were not a disaster [2.0 for 12 hours: D - C - B - C] but I knew I could do a better job. Yeah, I could do better if all this other stuff wasn't on my mind all of the time. I lack PEACE and really don't know how or where to find it.

This vignette is based on a true story. It was told to me by a young man with a good but troubled heart. His story is indicative of the many stories being lived out in our society today. Young men, raised by a single mother, lacking a male influence. Young men are being raised without the perspective and counsel of older men who are living out the scenario only a few steps ahead. This male perspective is critically important for the survival and the success of our young people in a country full of racist, prejudicial, and uncaring individuals. Many times the father, or father figure, is in place, but fails to impart the knowledge and skills needed to move forward in our society. Instead we, at least a strong majority of us, continue to fall prey to the many overt and covert messages designed to help create fatalistic mind-sets within our society. James is now a gangbanger. As of this writing, he is recovering from a gunshot wound in the side of his chest.

These negative images of the African American and other subgroups of color, when acted out, create in the minds of many individuals representing mainstream America the notion that African Americans are not as capable as or as smart as they are. Sadly, these negative images defer dreams, dreams which often, as in this case, explode. Read on as I attempt to extend this premise. I say again, one must pray for the young one.

3

OVERCOMING HISTORIC INEQUALITIES AND SOCIAL STEREOTYPES

> Modern life means democracy, democracy means freeing intelligence for independent effectiveness—the emancipation of mind as an individual organ to do its own work. We naturally associate democracy, to be sure, with freedom of action, but freedom of action without freed capacity of thought behind it is only chaos. If external authority in action is given up, it must be because internal authority of truth, discovered and known to reason, is substituted (Dewey, 1903, p. 193).

Currently much debate and research are focused on reasons why certain ethnic groups as a whole seem to more easily adapt and succeed within the mainstream of society (Fordham & Ogbu, 1986, Matute-Bianchi, 1986, Gibson, 1988, Wilson, 1990, Ogbu, 1992). John Ogbu's article, "Adaptation to Minority Status and Impact on School Success," presents a compilation of these thoughts which, in his opinion, "form the basis of the alternative framework presented here for understanding why some minority groups, such as African Americans have disproportionate and persistent problems in school adjustment and academic performance" (Ogbu, 1992, p. 287). Ogbu's premise is based on extensive ethnographic research. Findings support the idea that groups that emigrated to this country voluntarily have no "ambivalent-oppositional" feeling toward the dominant culture, trust the schools, see difficulties as temporary surmountable hurdles to be overcome rather than "markers" of difference to be maintained, and have "an educational orientation that strongly endorses academic success as a means of getting ahead in the United States" (Ogbu, 1992, p. 291). In contrast, Ogbu says "one finds in the communities of involuntary minorities, cultural models that make them skeptical of the fact that they can get ahead merely through mainstream beliefs and strategies, even though they verbally endorse education as a means of getting ahead" (p. 291). These groups feel varying degrees of opposition from the dominant culture, distrust the school system, see difficulties as permanent situations instituted by the dominant culture, and point to a history of documented events as proof for their way of thinking. Lastly, it was found that all minority groups have culturally patterned educational strategies that either enhance or inhibit school success. And, although voluntary immigrant groups generally have more strategies than involuntary immigrant groups, according to Ogbu's research, there are members of each group who will be more or less likely to make use of strategies that enhance school success.

This research suggests that educators may have misunderstood the factors most relevant in minority children's lives that impact potential success in school. Instead of limiting our focus on the schools, homelife, or some biological characteristic, it is suggested that an examination of historical and structural contexts is needed to better understand the lack of academic and social success. West and Eubanks and Parish speak to this issue: "To engage in a serious discussion of race in America, we must begin not with the problems of black people but with the flaws of American society– flaws rooted in historic inequalities and long-standing cultural stereotypes" (West, 1993, p. 3). "After all, the primary purpose of schooling is to maintain and replenish the culture of an existing social system . . . The first step to reform must be for Americans to accept, and be able to discuss without guilt or blame, that schooling in America is part of a cultural process that sorts by race, class and gender" (Eubanks Parish, 1993, p.54). It is suggested we must be able to objectively explore the root causes for our lack of success.

> Education within a pluralistic society should affirm and help students understand their home and community cultures. However, it should also help free them from their cultural boundaries. To create and maintain a civic community that works for the common good, education in a democratic society should help students acquire the knowledge, attitudes, and skills they will need to participate in civic action and to make society more equitable and just (Banks, 1992, p. 32).

The issue is often associated with one of trust, respect, and equality of membership. All individuals want to feel a sense of worth to themselves and to the society within which they live. They want to be afforded the same opportunities as others to attain desired goals and objectives. Many people in our society are not afforded these opportunities, sought after by all. Instead, what we often experience is the outcome of a systematic process that creates an atmosphere of superiority of the dominant group over other subgroups. The process reinforces beliefs, attitudes, and misinformation about subgroups. This misinformation, carried over generation to generation, thus becomes part of the thinking, conscious and unconscious, of both the oppressor and the oppressed. This method of institutionalized oppression impedes the transformation process.

> Knowledge is the key to getting where we need to go. The human being is actually transformed by what he knows, not passively by just the potential. The human being is transformed by where his mind goes, not where his body goes. The human being is transformed by his thinking and not by his eating. The human being is transformed in a very special and unique way. This message of transformation is essential for the development of self-determination (Akbar, 1991, p. iii).

Even those individuals who have taken steps toward these goals and objectives are constantly reminded of the long road yet traveled. Cose (1993) sheds light on this premise:

> Notwithstanding currently fashionable arguments that blame white racism on black crime, it's unlikely that discrimination against certifiably "safe" blacks stems primarily from fear of black violence. Black executives, for instance, are not barred from private country clubs because white members fear their African-American peers will rob them. Nor do blacks associated in law firms have such difficulty advancing because white partners fear that black lawyers will rape their wives. Something other than anxiety over black crime is at work—something that lowering the black crime rate (desirable though that is) or even taking young blacks out of their environment (beneficial though that may be) will not necessarily change (pp. 12-13).

The desire for respect, trust, and equality of membership within the "Collective" is critical for the formulation of images of self-worth, visions of positive and productive life experiences and ultimately the internal strength of the society as a whole. The concept of the collective as the focal point for the development of strong societies, governments, institutions of learning, and other organizations committed to common goals can be traced back through history. When looking at groups of people, the basis for their union has generally centered around common ways of thinking or on the domination of one group over another. The destruction or dismantling of the group occurs when this common way of thinking is no longer a part of majority thinking or minority control. Voices (subgroups), traditionally undervalued in the collective have become extremely proactive toward the attainment of more meaningful input. Considering the demands for more innovation and productivity in today's marketplace, voices traditionally at the bottom of the well are beginning to attain leverage from which to gain the more meaningful input sought.

The concept of "otherness," people who are different in areas that include age, ethnic heritage, physical ability, religious belief, and sexual orientation, best describes the types of diversity which exist in our society. These areas of otherness help to create and interpret the environment each individual realizes. Life experiences, such as educational background, income, and religious belief of each individual, provide enhanced perspectives and thus are considered the essential elements of our beings and measures of our core identity. With this premise of a strong productive collective in mind, we can explore a more moral perspective that values, understands, and better utilizes our diverse societal membership.

THE POPULATION IN QUESTION

Children entering school today are different. The diversity of race, ethnicity, culture, socioeconomic standing, etc., continues to present new challenges for our schools.

> While the national population grew 9.8% during the 1980s, certain groups grew very rapidly, and others posted only small increases. The number of non-Hispanic whites grew by 6%; of African Americans, by 13.2%; of Native Americans, by 37.9%; of Asian-Pacific Islanders, by 107.8%; of Hispanics of all races, by 53%. (Hodgkinson, 1993, p. 620).

Probably the most critical factors associated with this growth in diversity is economics. The fastest growing population of poor people in this country is children. At the start of this year, "more than 23% of America's children were living below the poverty line and thus were at risk of failing to fulfill their physical and mental promise" (Hodgkinson, p. 620). Being poor in this country can take a tremendous toll on any individual, but especially on children. Poor children suffer from crime, unstable homes, child abuse, drugs, malnutrition, and many other negative factors associated with growing up and becoming who they are to a much higher degree than other children.

Consider the following:

> At the same time, however, a growing number of African-American parents with young children are experiencing chronic economic hardship and social isolation from extended family networks, stress factors that seriously undermine parenting and family functioning. Such parental stress and family dysfunction in turn contribute to the child's risk for school failure in at least two important ways. First, family dysfunction is associated with higher rates of child social—emotional problems and antisocial behavior, which contrib-

> ute to poor school adjustment (McLoyd, 1990; Patterson, DeBaryshe, & Ramsey, 1989). Indeed, the "difficult" temperamental dispositions found to be associated with school adjustment problems are considered to have their origins in disrupted early parent-child relationships. Second, such dysfunction disrupts the family's ability to provide emotional and instrumental support to the young child during the transition into schooling. These children, then, are truly "at risk," because they lack the family protective mechanisms necessary to allow them to meet the social and academic challenge of early schooling (Taylor, 1991, p. 19).

A life filled with so much uncertainty, violence, sadness, lack of structure and lack of love has a tremendous effect on the child's ability to function well in highly structured school settings guided primarily by state and local mandates that typically fail to address their ways of thinking and learning.

CASE IN POINT

Joseph it is your turn, please tell the class what exciting things you did over spring break.

Well, I figured out seven different ways to get home from school.

That's different, but Joseph, you live just three blocks from school. Why did you spend your break thinking of seven different ways to go home?

Some big boys jumped me about two weeks ago and beat me up on my way home. After about two or three times, I decided to change the way I went home. Instead of going straight home, (Joseph lives directly in front of the school, three blocks down), I went down to Trent street (one block down) and came around the back way and slipped in my house right behind them. This worked for about three days. After that they figured out what I was doing and so the boys caught me

> and beat me up again. Sometimes I would choose the right way, but sometimes they would still get me. So all last week I did some figuring.
>
> First I figured out as many ways as I could to go home from school and came up with seven different ways. Then I started thinking about when to use one of the seven ways to go home. I remembered how one of the big boys was always watching close to the school to see which way I headed home. When they saw me, they got me. So I will now fool them. I might start one way, but really go another way, or I might wait then sneak out another door from school. Anyway, I don't want to get beat up anymore by those sixth graders from the middle school. If this plan doesn't work, I plan on making friends with some seventh graders—for protection you know.

Before this discussion took place, Joseph was considered to be a low achieving second grader. His teacher, and the ones before in kindergarten and first grade, agreed with this opinion. Joseph's test scores indicated that he was behind in his reading skills by over one year. His school work and class activities seemed to demonstrate cognitive abilities in concurrence with his test scores, far below the "average" second grade student, (self-fulfilling prophecy?). Joseph, until now, had not demonstrated any abilities to analyze, synthesize, evaluate and reconceptualize anything. All of a sudden, this conversation demonstrates quite the opposite. Why?

Well, some would say this was just an accident, but others think not. The key to making this type of cognitive ability more the norm, they say, is to make the lesson relate to the student's everyday life experiences. Joseph was able to bring forth these skills because the situation was important to him. The scenario presented a real-life application for processing desired outcomes.

THE HIDDEN CURRICULUM

Schools often communicate a "hidden curriculum" that further complicates an already disheartening situation. It is a hidden curriculum often in conflict with publicly espoused philosophies concerning the teaching/learning process and endorsed goals and objectives. A hidden curriculum steeped in tradition, often due to habits and beliefs formed from birth, manifesting itself both consciously and unconsciously. A hidden curriculum reinforcing certain values, social interaction, ideological orientations, and theoretical concepts directing teaching and learning processes often detrimental to children "outside" of mainstream America. Often this hidden curriculum sets standards (social competencies) by which the measure of a student's level of success in school can be significantly influenced. These social competencies begin to influence the students' perceived level of acceptance from day one. When behavioral characteristics and ways of negotiating the environment are at odds with established norms and expectations (although often hidden) the cards begin to be stacked, and patterns of school failure are set in motion. Students' ability to negotiate these sets of cloaked standards depends to a great extent on their level of success in developing interpersonal relationships with teachers in the school settings. Becoming skilled in the ability to demonstrate social competence in the classroom enhances the student's self-esteem and sense of self-efficacy, which then enhances the student's commitment to the teaching/learning process and motivation for learning growth.

A lack of social competence is often associated with lower teacher expectations, less student productivity and academic growth, and even more behavioral problems in the classroom.

This type of philosophical ideology supports the premise that failure rests primarily on the student. This mind-set rarely objectively considers the outcomes of such a destructive philosophy—outcomes considered by many to be at the core of our societal concerns today. And even more rarely does it consider good teaching based on the use of divergent thinking and the use of varied activities and instructional approaches to enhance the potential for success of ALL students. The call for social, political, and economic considerations and adjustments as a means for creating growth opportunities in this context for students is often summarily dismissed or addressed only slightly as a form of mere accommodation and appeasement. Generally, teachers tend to prefer and have more positive attitudes toward students who fit the existing square hole. Students fitting in round holes, or triangular or three-dimensional holes are often seen as too problematic and are not provided appropriate opportunities for academic and social growth. "Just throw the dog a bone, leave the meat for us. After all, that's all he can really handle anyway."

It is suggested here that a more positive and productive approach to successful teaching and learning begins with welcoming diversity. The thoughts of Loden and Rosener (1991) on diversity are enlightening:

> Like trees in a vast forest, humans come in a variety of sizes, shapes, and colors. This variety helps to differentiate us from each other. While we share the important dimension of humanness with all members of our species, there are biological and environmental differences that separate and distinguish us as individuals and groups. From an objective point of view, it is this vast array of physical and cultural differences that constitute the spectrum of human diversity. From

> the subjective point of view, diversity is otherness or those human qualities that are different from our own and outside the groups to which we belong, yet present in other individuals and groups (p. 18).

Diversity can best be described as a concept that embraces the broad range of ethnic, linguistic, religious, racial, sexual, socioeconomic and cultural differences that exist or may exist in society. Upon further examination, diversity includes elements based upon such things as preferential, prudential, aesthetic, religious, and ethical positions, beliefs, and judgments. These differences, along with philosophical and paradigmatic disagreements, have a tremendous impact on school settings, and on the chosen path instruction will travel. Therefore, those voices that have historically been at the bottom of the socioeconomic, political, and academic will continue, for the most part, to be ignored. As we move into the twenty-first century, priority must be placed on finding ways to prize and utilize the new diversity that exists. The diversity in the ways students experience life and acquire knowledge will continue to challenge every teacher's ability to be successful.

4

RETHINKING WHAT SCHOOLS DO

I've come to a frightening conclusion that I am the decisive element in the classroom. It's my personal approach that creates the climate. It's my daily mood that makes the weather. As a teacher, I possess a tremendous power to make a child's life miserable or joyous. I can be a tool of torture or an instrument of inspiration. I can humiliate or humor, hurt or heal. In all situations, it is my response that decides whether a crisis will be escalated or de-escalated and child humanized or dehumanized (H. Ginott).

This following vignette is typical of conversations between teachers in many of our schools, especially in our urban schools.

A. Another week! I just do not understand these kids! They just don't care about school. I can't get them to work in class and never, ever have homework returned.

B. I know what you mean. I don't even assign homework anymore. These kids just do not want to learn!

A. Sometimes I think they might want to do a good job, but maybe they just can't do it. Anyway, I've paid my dues down here—it's time to get out and teach some real students. I mean kids that want to learn, with parents that understand the value of an education, the kind of families across town.

B. I'm with you. If they don't acknowledge my transfer this

year, I'm applying in the suburbs. I've given it my all. Just like you, I have tried to adjust my teaching. These kids are slow, I know, so I've worked hard at modifying lessons to make things easier. But how slow and low do you go?

A. Me too, but when test scores tell you how far behind they are, just what do they expect, miracles? We just cannot compete and they know it!

B. Well, I really don't blame the kids. After all, they are "at risk." They are so poor and most have only one parent. I just don't understand why these women put up with such sorry men.

A. Yeah, and drugs are all over the place. I even heard that many of our mothers sell themselves so that they can buy more drugs. Kids are left alone at home all night. They have to feed, clean and clothe themselves almost every day.

B. I think some of them need help when it comes to cleaning themselves.

A. My husband hates the thought of me driving through this neighborhood.

B. I think some of my kids must be crack babies. I mean they just stare into space at times like they're so bored. At other times they can't sit still for two minutes! I've had enough of this lunacy.

A. Or maybe it's Attention Deficit Disorder. Something is wrong and it's not me!

B. Right, it's not me either.

C. What about the work I saw this morning around your walls?

A. That was done at Saturday school here.

B. It's real good work. I see a lot of critical thinking and creativity in many of those writing samples.

A. I agree, the work is excellent. But like I said, that work was done in Saturday school, where all they do is have fun.

B. I really thought our in-service sessions at the end of last year and the start of this school year would help us with these kids.

A. Which ones? Learning styles or whole language? I thought both were excellent.

B. I was thinking more about our sessions on cooperative learning and developing interdisciplinary lessons.

A. It really doesn't matter what we try, they just don't get it! I really doubt if they're able to learn what's important. They can learn the lyrics of any rap song in no time, but when it comes to real knowledge, these kids, maybe it's just too hard for them. I've tried all forms of everything my mind can think of and more. But look at what we've got to work with. Tell me—well it's just time for some more fresh meat. After all, this is good training ground. I've paid my dues and it's time to be "movin on up." Darn, there's the bell, another week of this crap.

B. I have begun to hate Sunday evenings because of this, another week with them. I can't even sleep on Sunday nights. This has got to be my last year here.

A. Mine also, even if it means changing careers. I've been checking into becoming a firefighter.

Teachers expressing these and similar concerns seem to want success but feel helpless. Their lack of success and feelings of helplessness have been a feeding ground for frustration and anger.

Why such little success? Are poor showings in direct relation to inferior students, poor teaching, ineffective leadership, societal apathy, or parent apathy? Many individuals would probably suggest that each of these factors, and others, play a role in this lack of student and teacher success.

MENTAL SYNTHESIS

People do not ordinarily loathe themselves. As a matter of fact, human history is replete with numerous instances of peoples who considered themselves *the people nonpareil*, which is to say unique in the creative scheme of things. Certainly it would be difficult to imagine an Ashanti or Yoruba warrior fresh off the slave ship at Charleston at war with himself over his identity; and if Nat Turner, David Walker, or Harriet Tubman had any such anxieties, *even after the experience of slavery*, they were the best-kept secrets of the age. Self-loathing is a counter function to survival and to the will to survive. It must therefore be considered abhorrent to any natural human predisposition. In consequence, if people do not come into the world hating themselves, then self-hatred, wherever it exists, must be a learned response, an acquired pattern of behavior, a dysfunctional contaminant from the human flux in which one's primary socialization takes place. Hence, it is reasonable to look for the origins of self-hatred outside the group in which it is alleged to occur, and more specifically, inside any associated group which stands to be convenienced by it (Lincoln, 1993, p. 198).

To turn failure into success, curriculum must become a focal point. Meanings, how we define ourselves and others, are interpreted and structured into curriculums. Some believe that curriculum design should focus on whose knowledge is most important, who should decide on what knowledge should be taught, how knowledge should be taught, and why. Others understand that truth is subjective—based on our personal experiences and the experiences of our society. In other words, they see and believe that knowledge is not constant. However, the dominant Anglo societal leadership have stated that Western European knowledge is most important; that this knowledge, if not exclusive, will be of primary importance, that the premise of the teacher as expert and student as empty vessel, in part, drives methodologies. And why? Because it is.

Historically subgroups, or groups considered outside of mainstream America, have not experienced equal membership in the educational process. Some call this form of curriculum design selective tradition. A process of selecting, from a whole possible area of past and present, certain meanings and practices for emphasis while certain other meanings and practices are neglected and excluded. Recent concern for what some call gross injustices in curriculum design have reached, in some opinions, critical mass. The masses are angry, they want equality, they demand equality. This pattern has existed throughout the history of curriculum development in this country.

In *Inside Out: Contemporary Critical Perspectives in Education,* Elizabeth Ellsworth writes:

> The CANONS [a body of principles, rules, standards, or norms] of all traditional academic disciplines in the West were institutionalized during times of violent and blatant racism, sexism, colonialism, and exploitation of human and natural resources. People working in the new disciplines mentioned above [ethnic studies] have demonstrated how official curriculums and "the canon" continue to naturalize, justify, and extend those dynamics into what is taught in schools and how it is taught (Ellsworth, 1994, p. 101).

What is most taught often minimalizes the efforts and contributions of subgroups. Rather, the group in control, the dominant group, has made continual efforts to enhance, primarily through education, their place as first and utmost in the world.

Thomas A. Parham tells us that:

> These efforts of control and domination make perfect sense if one understands that the principles and practices of oppression are primarily psychological in nature. Thus, the control over physical space (geography), modes of production (labor), and the educational and religious indoctrination of a people all involve a reformation of the psyche of the oppressed victim. The consequence is the deliberate construction of the psychologically rooted political, economic, social, educational, and religious systems which are designed to guarantee the survival of the White race and place them (Whites) at the center of the world. Also, given the Eurocentric propensity for dichotomous thinking (either/or) and a belief in a "difference equals deficiency" logic, African Americans have been and may always be on the negative end of any conceptual analysis provided by Europeans, regardless as to whether the polarities represent good-bad, best-worst, or su-

perior-inferior (Parham,1993, p. III).

Curriculum constructionists understand the notion that ideas implanted in the mind are strong influences on the type of behavior exhibited by students.

> The struggles and analyses of people who have been exploited and made invisible by dominant meanings of "woman," "poor," "black," "disabled," "gay," or "lesbian," for example, have shown that the "foundations" and canons of academic disciplines do not represent neutral "facts" or a pre-given "reality." Rather, they represent the experiences, desires, and political interests of the social and cultural groups that were in the position to name and shape the histories, experiences, and meanings of their own and other social groups. The argument that meaning is the product of social and political interaction seriously undermines a number of claims that support dominant Western thought and education. These include claims that there are absolute universal truths that can be known, that there are single indentifiable origins and causes of events, that there is an essential and common human nature or experience, that there are universal human goals, and that a utopian future that benefits everyone can be envisioned. The image of the scientist or educator as one who speaks with certainty, authority, and a single "correct" perspective from which to represent the world is under serious attack by those who have suffered under institutionalized scientific and educational authority (Ellsworth, 1994, p. 102).

Efforts to stimulate success in schools must be directed toward redesigning curriculum. An evolving curriculum dedicated to eliminating the control and domination of one group; where trust, value and equal membership of all groups making up our society are focal points of concern.

TEACHER PREPARATION

> A teacher is very much like a business consultant. During the fact-finding phase the consultant researches the people, culture, and goals of the organization. The consultant then identifies the problems and issues confronting the organization before recommending possible solutions. Teachers develop effective lesson plans and teaching strategies through an in-depth understanding of their students, their community, and the obstacles and issues that uniquely pertain to them. Even an understanding of these factors represents a moving target. Teaching strategies must change as people, communities, schools, and the times change (Wynn, 1991, p. 1).

To turn failure into success, it is suggested here that the teacher become a focal point. Most of us are in some way involved in preparing individuals to become successful and competent leaders in the teaching/learning process. Our students will be charged with educating children whose ways of interacting with the environment are at times quite different from what they have been adequately trained to handle or have experienced during their formative days in schools.

> When significant changes and shifts in curriculum and instruction occur in teacher preparation, the potential exists for particular and long-term impact on society. Teacher candidates, especially those in undergraduate teacher preparation programs, acquire subject matter knowledge and also, unlike those in other professions, learn about the structure of the disciplines and approaches to their professional work. What curriculum and what instruction they experience influence what and how they will teach. As the persons beyond the family who are uniquely charged with the responsibility of

> enculturation (Goodlad, 1990), teachers are the major actors in the process of cultural and social reproduction. Students in teacher preparation programs will transmit the values, attitudes, and patterns of interaction in their work with individuals and groups. They will interpret for their students what are the negative and positive sanctions of various orientations and behaviors of the wider society. What happens in their studies in college is critical to the society at large. And, of course, who they are and what educational and cultural histories they come to college with are the lenses through which college experiences are understood (Francis-Okongwu & Pflaum, 1993, pp. 112-113).

Therefore, it is of major import that we help our future teachers maintain open-minded attitudes and develop the types of reflective practices needed to monitor, evaluate, and revise continually their own teaching practices. Only then will they be able to create and maintain environments that foster better understanding of the students they will be teaching. Only then will they be able to help students understand themselves. All too often students are asked to repeat words, use ready-made materials selected and organized by the teacher or curriculum designers, and talk about ideas with little to no depth of understanding of concepts presented. This type of learning, measured by the student's ability to repeat certain phrases and formulas, lacks motivational incentive for students to internalize information. What evolves is a teaching/learning environment that undermines attempts by students to adequately grasp meaning and content. Therefore, perhaps, a succession of experiences and interactions closely connected to student life experiences would enhance curricula. Providing students with opportunities to select and organize materials, thus including them (students) in the bridge-building process, might prove beneficial to the improvement of schools. It is thought some formula including these ideas would cause a higher degree of internalized motivation in students.

Or, do we continue to make attempts at fitting new demands (diversity of student population) into existing boxes? The notion is to view knowledge as a much more flexible, fluid product of people's experiences and thus to value this concept as a critical progression toward enhancing the teaching/learning environment for higher levels of student success. Educators must believe in the premise that it is not only what the teacher does, but also what the teacher gets the student to do and understand that is most important. The Holmes Group (1990) expressed concern for this issue:

> "Schools need to do a much better job of building on students' own cultural capital. Teachers will have to become closer students of their own students. A pluralistic democracy whose schools are full of immigrant children and children from many peoples and races requires teachers prepared to become more thoughtful about Culture in another sense: cherishing and building on the webs of meaning and value and community that students bring to school. We see the schools as building bridges between traditional academic culture, the culture of students, and world culture" (p. 17).

CONCLUDING THOUGHTS ON THIS ISSUE

Calls for changes in our educational system generally bring focus to content, pedagogy, or the organizational structure. While changes in each of these areas can improve the quality of education and should be considered, it is suggested here that limited gains, if any, will be achieved if the issue of community and, within this notion, the valuing of others are not primary concerns. Haberman (1991, pp. 293-294) describes a quality teaching/learning environment as one in which students are involved with:

(1) issues they regard as vital concerns;
(2) explanations of human differences;
(3) major concepts, big ideas, and general principles, not merely isolated facts;
(4) planning what they will be doing;
(5) applying ideals such as fairness, equity, or justice to their world;
(6) activity rather than passivity;
(7) real-life experience;
(8) heterogeneous groups;
(9) questioning assumptions, relating new ideas to old ones, or applying learning to life;
(10) redoing, polishing, or perfecting work; and
(11) the technology of information access.

When reviewing the eleven components Haberman recommends, a critical concept can be noted time and time again that identifies the type of environment most conducive to successful teaching and learning in many of our schools today and as we prepare for the twenty-first century. That concept requires teachers to embrace the concept of community within diverse settings, thus providing a pathway for the bridge building which is essential for the level of student academic and social growth needed to help keep our society [community] strong.

We must dedicate ourselves to providing future educators

with the ability to fill gaps, to build paths over depressions, to surmount obstacles, with the result of making the teaching/learning process more realistic to the student. The foundations for this type of bridge building are the connections we make with students' existing life experiences. Making these types of connections helps to make the learning meaningful to our students. It provides that pathway we seek to successfully connect what teachers want students to know with what they already know. We must embrace the concept of community. The word community is historically related to the Latin *communis* and implies something that is "shared, common, general, universal, public" (Simpson, 1959, p.121). When applied to people, it also suggests that one is "approachable, not pretentious, affable" (p. 121). When employed in connection with a group or society, the word connotes something that is accomplished "for the public good, for common use" (p. 121). Collectively, these thoughts reflect the notion that a community of teachers and administrators share something in common for the good of society, including their students and their own microcommunities, the school and classroom. A hypothetical illustration follows:

> Jody Creamer is a seven-year veteran teacher with an outstanding teaching record, all of which was in a small rural school district in Montana. She moved with her husband after his promotion required them to relocate to a large city in Texas. She is currently in her first year in this large urban school district, at an elementary school with a student population that is 99.9% African-American and .1% Hispanic. Her fourth-grade class is all African-American. Mrs. Creamer understands the essential elements her state and district mandate as minimum skill objectives and makes extensive use of the district's curriculum guides when developing lesson plans.

Her fellow fourth-grade teachers generally agree that Jody writes very good lesson plans, is creative in her approach to the teaching/learning process, wants to be successful, and is very concerned about her lack of success. She just cannot figure out why motivating her students to actively engage in the learning seems to be such a monumental task. During a recent discussion with her principal, Jody described a lesson which she thought was outstanding, yet the lesson seemed to lessen rather than pique the interest of many students, creating an atmosphere of forced [prison-like] activity.

"I told my students that today we were going to begin to learn how to give a speech. I provided an introduction by using part of a great oration of one my favorite speakers, former President Jimmy Carter. I then provided a similar example using a recorded speech of our mayor on the subject of the new arts district during last month's re-election campaign. We then had an exercise emphasizing critical elements to speech making which called for a large amount of student participation. I then read a speech that I had made when in the fourth grade. This speech, by the way, won first place back in my home town of Ocean, Montana. Students were then asked to practice reciting this speech and told that they would be graded on the critical elements discussed at the end of the week. Each day we worked on the speech during our language arts block. Although most of my students actually memorized this short speech, very few repeated it with any emotion or emphasis, especially at critical moments. Even fewer students could remember my explanation of what message I was trying to relay [the ideal family] in the speech! Needless to say, I was once again in a quandary. What am I doing wrong or not doing right?"

Mrs. Creamer's principal, Mr. Helpmaster, suggested, in reteaching this lesson, that she could still use the examples previously given, but to follow them with examples of speeches her students could identify with more. He suggested that she include a speech by Rev. Dr. Martin Luther King, Jr., Jose Rojas (the school board president), and the recent speech given at the last PTA meeting by our sixth-grade oratorical winners. Mr. Helpmaster then suggested that she allow her students to identify critical elements in each speech, maybe using an inquiry method of instruction. Students should then be allowed to write their own speeches, recite them, and talk about what each meant to them. This method of instruction, he said, would invite the students into the learning process. It would provide students with a means of expressing themselves in an atmosphere that valued their experiences and ways of interpreting the way they interact with the environment while at the same time providing them with valuable information to improve both their academic and social growth. He told Mrs. Creamer that it was extremely important to keep in mind the issue of relevance when teaching. He stated, "We must remember that part of our job is that of bridge builders. We build bridges to connect what students already know with what we want them to know. This is the fundamental premise our foundation of listening, caring, valuing, and welcoming the many young, voices speaking to us is built on. We make decisions and act on the belief that we are viable, competent, and important individuals, all able and willing to make positive contributions to the society within which we live, if given the chance."

Yet, many teachers consider the prior knowledge of some students as detrimental to new learning. These teachers choose to under-utilize or at best ignore perceived prior knowledge deficiencies.

The idea that learners bring group and individual histories

> into the classroom is not new. Bloom (1976) has noted that the individual characteristics that learners bring to a task may set the stage for further learning and performance. Every learner brings to the task a prior history of learning and ways of doing. For African Americans, these entry characteristics are thought to include a preference for people-oriented situations and a highly affective orientation toward ideas, people, and things (Boykin & Toms, 1985; Shade, 1982; Young, 1974). An examination of the cultural patterns of socialization that many African-American children experience in their families and the typical classroom environment encountered by these children in elementary school suggest potential conflict between learner and task environment (Nelson-LeGall & Jones, 1991, p. 35).

Many times we assess students as they enter school, find deficiencies based on a set of norms valued by mainstream America, and then use this information to pass judgment as to a student's ability to learn. Often it is not their ability to learn that we uncover, but rather their readiness to learn what we want them to learn in the way we want them to learn it. It must be remembered that we all work harder to understand something when we see how that something connects with our reality and is therefore important.

Therefore, more evaluators must begin to reflect on current practices and be prepared to make the type of adjustments conducive to higher levels of student success.

> Changing the structure of schools means re-conceptualizing how learning takes place, questioning whether all students benefit from rigid and self-contained classrooms, investigating whether meaningful connections are being made among the discrete subjects which young people experience, and creating conditions that help students whose motivation and

achievement are stymied, return to productive learning. These are responsibilities of leaders who want to expand the environment for learning so all students will be well-served by elementary and secondary schools in the United States (Nieto & Sinclair, 1991, pp. 49-50).

5

THE ROLE OF LEADERSHIP

A democratic society is, in part, one built on a foundation of trust and respect—a society in which individuals actively seek to respect the thoughts and opinions of others. This society embodies a proactive philosophy designed to make positive use of the diversity of thoughts, feelings and actions for the good of the many, not the one. It is a society in which members strive to develop their potential, seeing lifelong learning as key to the society's continued existence. If these expressed beliefs are not producing the desired results, then we must look for the reasons that human beings are treated differently. Becoming sensitive to existing conditions and no longer perpetuating current practices can be a starting point toward creating new pathways of understanding for all people.

Knowledge becomes the concrete forming this foundation of trust and respect. When educators embrace this premise, the mission to help develop the minds of all students travels along a pathway free of many existing barriers.

> In a democracy, the good life is not living in leisure and luxury. It is a life in which one is continually developing understanding of man and society and the environment which contributes to man's growth or which inhibits it. It is a life in which one is continually developing actions appropriate and effective in helping others to attain the good life. It is a life in which one is continually developing increased enjoyment and appreciation of beauty in people and in their actions. The conception strongly emphasizes continuing development. This

means life-long learning, avoidance of a plateau in development, and the avoidance of regression. It also means helping others lead the good life; helping all others with whom one has opportunity for significant contact without regard to the usual barriers of race, gender, religion, or ethnic origin (Tyler, 1991, pp. 9, 17).

Leadership, therefore, focuses energy toward the development of the unique interests, attitudes and knowledge base of each individual. This focus, when successful, draws on the assets of each person, thus taking advantage of a major strength, maybe *the major strength*, this nation has always possessed, the **diversity** of its citizenry.

This premise requires that leaders must view their environments not as separated from the educational system, but as intricately interwoven with it into an evolving reality that will one day be our future. No longer can leaders afford simply to perpetuate an existing order; they must become, instead, proactive, dedicated shapers of a future reality committed to the principles of human decency.

The comments of Barnett, McQuarrie, and Norris support this premise.

> "We believe that the moral imperatives of leadership demand that leaders seek to understand present conditions and that, in reflecting, they dare to question existing practices. We believe that moral leadership must be sensitive to the human condition and seek to create new avenues of understanding for all people. . . In short, we contend that our educational system, and especially its leaders, must focus attention on how human beings are treated and the moral decisions that determine our actions" (1991, p. 6).

Leadership in our society has, throughout history, demonstrated the capacity to create, control, and/or embellish premises concerning varying elements and subgroups which make up the citizenry. These activities can either enhance or diminish the levels of social and intellectual achievement of a given organization, idea, or subgroup. Often particular subgroups have been, and continue to be, targeted for negative imaging.

Many events have helped to shape the concept of collegiality in this society. The American society, its businesses, institutions, and ways of thinking, began being shaped by the values and experiences of western European white men. The norms, behaviors, traditions and expectations that continue to have a major influence on all segments of our society were planted by these "founding fathers."

An ethnocentric/Eurocentric approach was institutionalized during this time. This approach generates concepts of superiority over others whose ways of thinking, knowing, and interacting with the environment are different from those of western European traditional mind-sets. This devaluing of others, now making up a substantial percentage of America's tapestry, has historically limited opportunities for growth and full societal inclusion. Instead of welcoming diversity in areas of our society, we have a history of using the diverse ways of living and thinking of subgroups as a means of measuring self-worth. The human being's need for self-actualization has led to a system designed to enhance a particular group's level of control and prosperity at the expense of others, primarily through the negative propagation of differences. For example, cultural deprivation is based on the assumption that the standards of white middle-class America represent norms by which all other subgroups may be appropriately measured. If the norms of a particular subgroup fall short of these standards of expectation, this subgroup is considered culturally deprived. People and organizations believing in this cultural deprivation ideology tend to frame differences in language and behavioral styles as cognitive deficiencies. They believe linguistic competence to be synonymous with the development of standard English. They refuse to acknowledge any validity to the premise that, although their language system may be different, people outside of mainstream America are neither linguistically impoverished nor cognitively underdeveloped. The dominant culture fails to recognize the language system of these groups as being fully developed and highly structured. This does not mean that others should not be competent in speaking and writing standard English. After all, developing standard English abilities is critical to an individual's level of academic and social success in this society. However, these prevailing attitudes have had a tremendously negative effect on the concept of embracing diversity as a pathway for full equitable inclusion for all in our society.

LEADERSHIP AND THE SCHOOL PRINCIPAL

Role definitions for the principal are often impacted by societal expectations and constraints. Demands on the principal from forces both outside and inside the school, often capitulate toward currently existing societal issues. The principal attempts to function within a rapidly transforming society whose expectations are in a state of constant change. This transformation process is further complicated by the efforts of a multitude of voices wanting to provide input into what they think "should be" (Morgan, 1986; Sergiovanni, 1990).

Leadership helps to mold varying interests into a functionary unit--a school--in which all stakeholders feel a sense of ownership regarding desired outcomes (Buffie, 1989). This function of leadership, taking often divergent forces and creating a core of common goals, has been a major component of effective role definitions for the principal. Success here is closely associated with the kinds of relationships developed and maintained throughout this never ending process (Sergiovanni, 1990).

The needs of the many are more important than the needs of the few, or the one--this is a premise successful principals develop as a primary pathway for student success. This premise is built on a foundational relationship of trust and respect between principal and teacher, teacher and students, principal and student, and all other combinations of school stakeholders. A school organization in which individuals actively seek to respect the thoughts and opinions of others and unselfishly seeks common ground enhances the transformation process. This becomes a proactive philosophy designed to make positive use of the variety of thoughts, feelings and actions for the good of the many, in this case all of our students and all individuals making-up our society (Norris, 1994).

Leadership, therefore, focuses energy toward the development of the unique interest, attitude and knowledge base of each individual. This focus, when successful, draws on the assets of each person, thus taking advantage of a major strength, the power of unity of thought and unity of action.

Attempts to develop unity of thought and unity of action can be further complicated by the level of diversity which exists in many of our schools today. Value systems are present within each individual, many having or developing powerful voices. These values are used as measures by which relationships are formed and transformed.

The Role Of Leadership

> The formation and positive transformation of relationships between teachers and principals is further complicated by beliefs each individual brings with him or her to the school environment (Blase & Kirby, 1992; Scott, 1987).

Therefore, the principal's perceptions, or how he/she interprets varying teacher-principal interactions, play a major role in the development of the type of relationships desired for school success. Individuals often interpret their interactions with others based on previous experiences. These past experiences, both negative and positive, either enhance the positive transformation of relationships or provide barriers to it. A recent study by this author attempted to unearth specific barriers facing African American principals and their Anglo teachers with regard to building toward a collective mind-set. Questions designed to expose assumed barriers were developed and presented to practicing African American principals supervising Anglo teachers in school populations made up predominantly of African American students. The results were somewhat surprising and yet some would say very inspiring. There are at least two possible ways of looking at this phenomenon. One, among educators, unlike many other domains of adult interaction, race neither divides colleagues nor interferes with a complex, shared task. Of course, at this point, we have only the appointed leaders' statements to that effect, and they would presumably be highly motivated to show themselves as "in charge" and their schools as free of racial tensions or dysfunctional relationships. Indeed, the ethic of leadership especially in education would seem to suggest ignoring or avoiding racial tensions unless impossible. After all, the dominant ethic of all educators is that "We're all in it for the children."

So, we can question whether tension-free relationships and

acceptance of African American leadership are part of the ideology of administration, and perhaps a desire to believe, contrary to West's perspective, that race does not matter among people of good faith and shared goals. But that questioning may just stem from skepticism and experience–it is not after all well-supported by these principals' reports (who were promised anonymity and informed that this was not a district-sponsored project). Thus, one must consider the obvious conclusion: These answers honestly reflect the beliefs among these educators, all of whom lead racially mixed faculties teaching predominatly minority student populations.

There are some who argue that the dominant aspect of education as a career is its moral demands and dimensions, that the characteristic personal equality of career educators is a moral commitment to the lives of children. Teacher and administrator reports, even when teaching children different in race and ethnicity from themselves, <u>still</u> sound the same message: We do this for the children, their futures and prospects. Although race and class can create barriers to educator's sense of efficacy, it may not affect directly their commitment and shared faith. Even more, their belief that they <u>must</u> share that faith may overwhelm doubts and sustain bridges, even if they are occasionally shaky or imperfectly built.

What these principals may be expressing then is a doctrine of faith in their colleagues. And more importantly, in the process of schooling to overcome selfish adult barriers in the best interests of children. They believe an image of the school as a safe place where issues of race, while not inconsequential or irrelevant, are not critical fault lines in interpersonal relations. If not explicitly accurate perhaps, these beliefs are visionary in promoting images of settings where diverse groups of people gather each day to pursue a work which all conceive as too important to tolerate distractions. Cose addressed this in his book, *The Rage of A Priviledged Class*:

> Or, do responses of principals in this study support the findings of Eubanks and Parish (1993)."After all, the primary purpose of schooling is to maintain and replenish the culture of an existing social system...The first step to reform must be for Americans to accept, and be able to discuss without guilt or blame, that schooling in America is part of a cultural process that sorts by race, class and gender." Are we sticking our heads in the sand? Are we so focused on adapting in order to fit into the organizational culture that we forget how real, substantive change occurs?
>
> Many African Americans support the premise that raising issues of race, class and gender only disaffiliates those who think that racism is a thing of the past. They believe, "to acknowledge their race-related anger or frustration would be to alienate (and perhaps provoke reprisals from) those whites whose goodwill was essential to their well-being" (Cose, 1993, p. 31).

So, these same African Americans align themselves to the philosophical beliefs of individuals such as Alan Bloom, E.D. Hirsch, William Bennett, Mortimer Adler, Diane Ravitch, Lynne Cheney, and Dwight Murphey who see the concept of valuing others as, ...the most serious impending challenge to American and European society, and indeed to free civilizations (Murphey, 1991, p. 33).

Historically, those most vocal about expressing their anger have been labeled malcontent or maladjusted persons, clearly not worthy of more (and perhaps deserving even less) responsibility within the organization. Yet some believe we must begin to actively explore this notion of schooling as a cultural process of social constructivism.

If all of our students are to be afforded opportunities to demonstrate the levels of success we claim to want, do we understand that significant change will come only when significant changes in the cultural effects of schooling take place? In other words, is there an opinion that race in this society, along with class and gender, plays a critical role in the quality of education delivered to individuals?

Or, should individuals espousing this type of ideology be considered, as Kristol and others believe, anti-American?

> It is in its most intense and extreme form . . that multiculturalism is on its way to being a major educational, social and eventually political problem.... [It is being] propagated on our college campuses by a coalition of nationalist-racist blacks, radical feminists, gays and lesbians, and a handful of aspiring demagogues who claim to represent various ethnic minorities. In this coalition, it is the Blacks who provide the hard core of energy, because it is they who can intimidate the faculty and administration, fearful of being branded as "racist." This coalition's multiculturalism is an ideology whose educational program is subordinated to a political program that is, above all, anti-American and anti-western . . [Advocates of this position] have now moved to an agenda of ethnic-racial conflict. [It includes] an effort to persuade minority students to be contemptuous of and hostile to America . . . interpreted as an age-old system of oppression, colonialism and exploitation . . It is now becoming . . . common within the American educational system for increasing numbers of young Blacks to learn that what we call "Western Civilization" was invented by Black Egyptians and feloniously appropriated by the Greeks, or that black Africa was a peaceful, technologically advanced continent before white Europeans devastated it (Kristol, 1991, p. 71).

However, if this opinion has merit, could it possibly provide focus to many of the concerns being addressed in our public schools today? Finally, is there hope for creating dialogue focused on true and often hidden agendas impacting our schools today? The concept of assimilation provides an example:

> Milton Gordon, in *Assimilation in American Life*, describes three distinct patterns of assimilation: Anglo-conformity, Melting Pot and Cultural Pluralism. Anglo-conformity was our traditional pattern and there is a clear concern that it has poorly served large numbers of our society and is a paradigm that needs to be replaced. For a long time the integrationist Melting Pot idea seemed the most viable alternative. . . Since 1970, however, it has slipped out of favor and is being replaced by Cultural Pluralism or multiculturalism. What is now occurring is a struggle between competing paradigms, with each one trying to discredit the other (Goldman, 1992, p. 61).
>
> The premise that education is the pathway by which this country will travel, be it a country road, boulevard, or interstate highway, can be greatly enhanced when our wagons no longer circle to protect the existing core when challenged, and instead, take positive steps to seek common ground. We should embrace a potentially painful, yet fruitful, renaissance in this nation. Rather than suppose that we emphasize differences between groups and demand enculturation, assimilation and accommodation of minorities with the establishment culture, transcultural education would emphasize the unity of cultures, the sameness of us all, and the need for tolerance and interdependence (Kierstead, 1992, pg. 223).

However, it seems some, including many public school African American principals, choose to deemphasize or lend a blind eye to these issues.

6

THE THREAT OF ASSIMILATION

> A growing body of evidence has demonstrated that there is a dynamic interaction between the human organism and its culture, and that it is impossible to abstract an individual's lifestyle from the culture that helps to mold it and through which it is expressed (Thomas & Sillen, 1992, p. 59).

Human beings become complex entities based on the effects of environmental inputs. For example, educational background, income, and religious belief help to mold the experiences of each individual. Because of these varying experiences, perspectives created provide for the complexity, and therefore the rationalization of the complexity, that exists today. The abundance of diverse perspectives on how individuals interact with the environment should naturally be reason for a means of productive and meaningful living. However, this obvious conclusion has managed to be an elusive concept in our American society. When a society fails in attempts to instill this type of collective mindset, violence becomes more prevalent, crime rates soar, homeless populations crowd downtown streets and underpasses. *The collective conscience becomes angry*—take a look around.

> It is suggested that a society determined to focus on a more moral perspective that values, understands, and better utilizes all of our diverse societal membership will experience the opposite—less violence, lower crime rates, fewer homeless

> people—a direction desired, if not by all, by most of us. "Believing in *a damn good chance* makes people feel energized and powerful. Believing in *no chance* makes people angry, passive, ineffectual. It may also make them violent" (Prothrow-Stith, 1991, p. 57).

Thomas and Simpson provide support for the need of a hard perspective.

> Creating environments conducive to growth, satisfaction, productivity, and effectiveness, if seen as a priority, can be facilitated by individuals, groups, and leaders who understand that tolerance of radical differences is not automatically an evil of contemporary institutions and society but can be a beginning plank in the bridge to a set of strong values that will enable us to span the differences themselves and to reach common ground on the other side. This kind of radical tolerance appears essential if we are to grow together and if we are going to come to greater mutual understanding and appreciation (Thomas and Simpson, 1994).

This issue of assimilation challenges results of the melting pot syndrome. Although many scholars believe in the premise of assimilation (like Mortimer Adler, William Bennett, Allan Bloom, E.D. Hirsch, Dwight Murphey, and Diane Ravitch), current actions demonstrate that this concept's attempt at creating a society of the many and the one, the pluribus and the unum, has debilitating effects on minorities, in particular African Americans. Individuals of this sub-group, more often than not, are forced to forget, ignore, or disguise their cultural heritage and concern for equal membership in order to gain partial acceptance and admittance into the societal mainstream. These differences in the way individuals perceive and interact with the environment are considered by some to be threats to the Union. Those most vocal about expressing their anger have historically been labeled malcontent or maladjusted persons. And their efforts declared anti-American, a danger to both our political and educational systems.

Often, proponents of assimilation seek to have others forget their differences by defining cultural, ethnic, religious, and other differences as inferior. They stress the need for unison of thought, unison of purpose, unison of voice, with *their* thoughts, *their* purpose, and *their* voice being the only one of importance.

> "The need for a past, for roots may be essential for all people, but it may have been overemphasized at the expense of hope for the future. Unlike trees, humans do not die without roots, but, as Scripture says of the future, "without hope the people perish." The "root" metaphor should be extended by the realization that although the trees in the forest - - elm, oak, birch, maple, etc. - - have different kinds of roots, they all depend upon a common soil, a common atmosphere and a common sun (Goldman, 1992, p. 61).

The melting pot or assimilationist view of a collective mindset does not allow for trust, respect and equality of membership for all its citizenry. It creates an atmosphere of hostility and violence, the type all too prevalent today. Its hierarchical structure employs barriers that allow only certain subgroups varying degrees of access to what is considered the fruits of full citizenship.

Thomas and Simpson write:

> Pseudo-tolerance, or tolerance that is based upon the falla-

> cious idea we must abandon any strongly valued differences, is unlikely to lead to cultural, ethnic, religious, and sexual inclusivism. This quasi-tolerance will result, not in equal respect of persons, social justice, community concern, political freedoms, and substantive distinctions, but in the resurrection of the old cultural and educational melting pot. Radical tolerance will create an environment for a cultural gumbo where every ingredient retains its distinct flavor while becoming part of the collective; quasi-tolerance will create an environment where covert and overt ways of eliminating cultural, ethnic, religious, and other differences are employed (Thomas and Simpson, 1994).

At one point, voices traditionally at the bottom of the well seemed to have some hope of grasping their piece of the American Dream. This seems to be a diminishing belief in many eyes today. Associated with an individual's sense of second-class citizenship is less identification with and involvement in the society, along with a lack of belief in and acceptance of the society's propagated goals and values. People become disenchanted—disenfranchised members whose hopes of achieving any part of the American Dream becomes a dream deferred, ready to explode. In fact, even many individuals who once thought they had achieved some degree of success in this endeavor, middle management types, have come to realize how it feels to move backwards (layoffs, cutbacks, downsizing, etc.), with little hope of regaining lost ground. You see, the collective is angry. The common ground essential for survival is eroding. Those visions and dreams of prosperity in America are turning into nightmares. Many individuals perceive a lack of respect, trust, and a high level of alienation within the societal power structure (this being very similar to the thoughts and attitudes of many individuals during the Revolutionary War, American Civil War, Bolshevik Revolution, French Revolution, Great Depression, and the recent demise of the Soviet Union). Historically, African Americans have experienced more barriers than other subgroups. However, due to over a decade of economic instability, voices traditionally infrequently valued in this collective have become extremely proactive toward the attainment of more meaningful input. Considering the demands for more innovation and productivity in today's international marketplace, voices traditionally at the bottom of the well are beginning to attain leverage from which to gain the more meaningful input sought.

There must be an asserted effort to turn many of the negative factors now in operation into positive vehicles for renewed prosperity and strength within our society. When inclusion takes the place of conformity as a focal point for equality, then and only then will a real, positive, and lasting commitment be afforded to all individuals seeking to define and discover the real fruits of life. We begin with strategy designed to promote the concept of embracing diversity. Valuing the ways others interact with the environment will then become a critical element essential for the desired results being sought by all.

> When young people feel that their lives are knit into the fabric of the society at large and when they face the future knowing that a fair share awaits them, they do not form or join violent gangs, although they do form social clubs, fraternities, sororities, and other age-mate groups. Violent gangs arise when young people face a future of limited opportunity and despair, when for military, political, social, or economic reasons the life that awaits a young person has been stripped of meaning and validity (Prothrow-Stith, 1991, pp. 96-97).

7

DREAMS DEFERRED

Now that we have discussed the many issues affecting our children's self-view and their educational experience, we can again ask: Why does our tiered educational system exist, and why does it have such negative effects on the poor, especially on African American males?

To answer this two-part question, we must address a premise that is currently, in varying forms, growing in acceptance as factual. Some would tell you that in a "democratic society," everyone cannot be rich, famous, intelligent, labeled as gifted in some way, college educated, considered at or near the "top of the hill," or president of the United States. Yet most, if not all of us, would describe life goals using some or all of these descriptions.

So the question becomes how can leadership create an environment that proclaims equal access to opportunities for all its citizenry in a free and open society, yet at the same time have as its true agenda social engineering? How can leadership create an environment in which tiers of social accomplishment can be somewhat attained without total anarchy from those individuals, historically African Americans, who ultimately end up at the bottom with little prospect of changing their plight in life? How can they escape from the bottom of the well, and if so, does someone replace them? Will there always be a bottom in this society? Or will perceptions of the "good life" become controlled by the individual, life, liberty and the pursuit of happiness, instead of by covert and overt institutional agendas? In other words, will we be able to play Monopoly without always being forced to go to jail without passing go in order to collect? Or always pulling Chance and Community Chest cards that impede instead of enhance personal goals of satisfaction while others seem to always avoid the go-to-jail path and manage to pull the right cards?

Well, for starters, leadership, it seems, develops a philosophy that values certain ways of interacting within a predetermined social structure. Leadership then allows only some people the opportunity to become a part of this philosophy. Leadership controls, as much as possible, levels of access to opportunity in numerous ways. Examples include forced assimilation, setting entrance criteria (barriers) against means of access (slavery, scientific propaganda, Jim Crow laws, inadequate education, testing), and monetary requirements for each phase. These and other methods are designed to inform, convince, brainwash the populace of their individual potential and that of others.

The primary problem with this system is that it is skewed—overbalanced in favor of the few, at the expense of the many. Barriers to access are not evenly distributed. African Americans, for example, experience more barriers, steeper hills and bumpier roads. Barriers, in the form of mental propaganda and poor educational opportunities, begin early in life. The following vignettes provide a brief look into examples of the experiences and thoughts of young African Americans living through some of the forms of mental propaganda.

SECOND RATE

How should I feel, at the age of nine, to know I am not welcome in places solely on the basis of my skin color? When individuals actively work toward defining themselves by making sure our opportunities are limited while theirs are limitless? We enter from the rear, if we enter at all. We drink from a different and dirty water fountain. As we walk in the rain to school, the school bus with the other kids passes us by and splashes mud all over us—the other kids laugh. The other kids laugh at us again as we pass their school, having another two miles before reaching our school. We start the new school year with old books, the ones used by the other kids for the last five years. Everything second-rate, at best. Does that make me second-rate too?

MY PARENTS

My parents seem to have two separate personalities. At home they are mostly happy and act as if they are in control, and they are. My father, at home, is strong and proud. My sisters and brother know who is king of this castle. My mother cooks, cleans and orders us kids around. They change, however, when around those other folk. My father no longer struts like a peacock. He walks with his shoulders humped, never looking them in the eye and only speaks when spoken to—yes sah or no sah. Sometimes my father laughs this crazy laugh around them, and at such corny jokes! He even makes us kids act differently. We must be very quiet, speak only when spoken to and never raise our heads eye level with theirs, only our eyes move up. My mother just seems to always be afraid around them. Are they stronger or better or smarter than us?

LINEAGE

Patrick could trace his lineage back to 15th century Ireland and even before that, he claims. I don't even know who my father was. I do know my mother and grandmother, but that's about it. I don't even know for sure if my grandmother was one of us or one of them. She was treated like one of us — so I guess she was.

Why are we treated so badly by them? Why do they know who their fathers were, and fathers' father and so on while I don't even know who my father was. Where is the fairness in that?

IMPRINTING

I was only seven, yet I remember the event as if it were today. He said he would not play with us, pointing to me saying, because he's a "Nigger."

INCIDENT

Once riding in old Baltimore
Heart-filled, head filled with glee,
I saw a Baltimorean
Keep looking straight at me.

Now I was eight and very small,
And he was no whit bigger,
And so I smiled, but he poked out
His tongue, and called me, "Nigger."

I saw the whole of Baltimore
From May until December;
Of all the things that happened there
That's all that I remember.

Countee Cullen

The other kids looked, then backed away from me. I didn't know what to do - - - so I just stood there and watched them play. They never asked me to play with them again. When I asked they would say, "We don't play with Niggers." So I stopped asking. Then they moved away.

LYNCHED

Lynched, that's what they called it—but what did it mean? I knew it was something bad. I knew it must have hurt. Everyone talked about it in whispers, with fright in their eyes. Some even shook and sweated like it was a hundred-degree day; it was more like twenty degrees. Somebody said, "They always stringin us up and a gettin' away with it." Another said, "You know there's a law for them and an unfair law for us—one they make up to fit their needs. As they continued, I figured out that lynching meant hanging—without any legal process preceding the event. They said it (the lynching) was done by some men in white hoods and robes—men that hated all of us, just because of our color. What's wrong with our color? What makes it so bad? Does it really make us bad? If not, then why do so many bad things keep happening to us?

JUST ANOTHER KID

They're just kids and so are we. But their parents won't let them play with us. Their parents call us no count "niggers" and "shines." They tell their kids, loud enough for us to hear, that they shouldn't play with the cursed of the earth, those half human darkies. One time I heard a parent tell her three boys that we were cousins to monkeys, just one step up. My mother told me to pray for these people. She said that they just needed to seek guidance from the Lord.

All that talk didn't hurt me though. I wish one of those bad talking men would call me a "nigger" or "shine" when I get grown! I'll just pop his eye out with my fist—that's what I'll do! Call me—talk about me like a dog! Just wait until I get grown!

BUSING

Busing began and all the other folk moved out. All the surrounding small towns became cities! Actually, the new businesses moving to the area, with jobs, located in these new cities (the suburbs). The other folk moved, now the jobs are moving too—away from us. Have you ever noticed the parks here and the parks closer to the suburbs? The parks near the suburbs are kept real clean. I think they take the trash and mowed grass from those parks and dump it in the parks around us. They certainly don't bother to come out here and mow or clean up.

We go out there (the suburbs) to work, but we better leave before dark! My cousin worked late one night and was stopped three times before making it to the freeway. His friend rides the bus. He was picked up at the bus stop and spent the night in jail because they said he looked like a thief they were looking for. He lost his job because he couldn't get out of jail until the next day and was late for work.

Almost as many people live in the suburbs now as in the city. They moved so their kids wouldn't be forced to go to school with us. Now they red-line so we can't live near them.

My cousin's friend, the one that was arrested? Well, it turned out that the guy they were looking for was five inches taller and sixty pounds heavier. He saw the description hanging over the shotgun in the front of the police car. They just picked him up because he was one of us!

ANGER

I hurt inside, all the way down to my ankles and all the way up to the back of my mouth. I'm bubbling—no, boiling inside with hate or confusion or—or I boil with a passion. My heart pounds. My breathing comes in heavy, short-jerky spasms. I grind my teeth, to stop, then start grinding away again. My fists clench so tight that only the tingly feeling of blood loss reminds me how tight I have become. I am mad —I hurt. I want to stop hurting but don't know what to do. All I keep telling myself is, this is the last time I take it, the last time the police harass me. They don't treat *them* like they treat *us*. This is the **last time**!

THE BERRY

Is it what they say man—the darker the berry, the sweeter the juice? Do they really go wild in the hay? I heard your women are the best, in the bed that is.

I wanted to do something to straighten the boys out. But I was so disappointed—no I was so angry. Just minutes before this happened I was thinking that some of them were okay. I thought that we could be close friends instead of just having a working relationship. I didn't want to lose my job either. So I told them it was just another one of those preconceived notions, a generalized notion that has been propagated by our society for years. I then excused myself to the restroom. I should have really set them straight!

FEELINGS

We were asked to close our eyes and reflect back to our childhood. At first I really couldn't become focused on anything. I was having a hard time finding something to report on when we opened our eyes, the required task — I hate these opening exercises. What I felt, and talked about, was the feelings generated during this reflective process. When thinking about my childhood, before starting school, I get this warm feeling. I know I was loved, cared for. Home, my parents, my family—what a nice place to be. I feel security, trust and a sense that everything is just fine. I miss those feelings now that my world no longer exists in such a warm safe environment.

THE EYES—LOOK AT HIS EYES

He came to our class one Monday afternoon. He was very quiet. When one looked at him, one would wonder whether or not he ever smiled. Such a sad look. I mean he smiled sometimes and even laughed once or twice. But his eyes, his eyes, how sad were his eyes. I also, or we, noticed his clothes. We often wore hand-me-downs, but his clothes were no more than thin rags. He had no coat and it was very cold these days. He had cardboard covering the holes in his shoes, there was more hole than sole, and he never had lunch or money to buy any. The kids began to treat him the way they treat us! Can you believe they would do such a thing? I mean we all knew how bad that made us feel. So I got beat up trying to stop all that stuff.

WE'RE ALL GOD'S CHILDREN

They send us across town by bus so we can, they say, integrate the schools and get to know each other. Now, they say the one-way 45-minute ride is worth the wealth of experiences gained. When we arrive at school, all of us go to rooms in the same wing of the building.

They say we are special so we need special help. I guess none of them are special. When we go to lunch, about 1:30, they have already eaten. I wonder if their food is cold and stale like ours. When we go to gym, or music or art, we go with each other and another group bussed in from close to our neighborhood. I think there are about 100 of us in the gym every Friday.

Man, the houses around this school look like mansions to us. They have real grass in their yards, too! I must admit, the school is much better than the one in our neighborhood. We have clean rooms with no roaches or rats. We have chalkboards you can really write on and see what you write. They say we have something called air conditioning. All I know is that it is really nice and cool inside when it's hot outside and real warm inside during the winter, and the ceiling doesn't leak water on me when it rains. We never had a school like this in our neighborhood. Our books look like new, and the library, wow, has so many books! But it's the last month of school and we still haven't gotten our turn to go to the library.

Each day as we load the bus for home, they look at us and we look at them, expressionless. Sometimes one of them might say something like, "Go home Niggers." Tell me, what kind of integration or rather desegregation is this?

THE POLICE

The police pulled us over; I was driving. They wanted to know where we were going. I asked them if I had done something wrong. I was so tired of being stopped all the time by the police for no reason. All they would do is detain, harass, and try to push us to the point of fighting.

One time a friend took the bait. He got so mad at a policeman's taunting that he took a swing at the cop. The officers laughed and beat my buddy to a pulp. They beat on him long after they had him down, I think he was unconscious. At least he wasn't moving and his eyes were closed. Blood was everywhere. When they finally got my friend to the hospital, the doctors noted a concussion, broken nose, dislocated shoulders, broken knee cap and numerous cuts and contusions. The police claimed resisting arrest. We said it was police brutality. They listened to the police.

Well, back to my original story. We were headed to the baseball game at Busch Stadium and told the police. So they detained and taunted us for awhile, like always. They would call us all kinds of names, talk about our mothers and did this so close to our faces that their spit sprinkled our faces. They knew what they were doing. They finally said we were no fun and let us go. By the time we got to the game it was the fourth inning. We looked at each other—but what could we do?

8

ANOTHER WAY TO SEE THINGS

What if, one day, there came to light irrefutable evidence that the philosophical principles on which this country, the United States of America, was built could be traced back to African origins? And how would perspectives change or shift if evidence for this argument could, in part, be debated via symbols on our dollar bill? Think about it. The debate might include the following facts.

Let us consider the fact that the "Founding Fathers" of this nation brought from Europe the concepts, ideologies, and practices of Freemasons and as a matter of fact were themselves Freemasons. The study of astrology and other ancient metaphysical sciences was emphasized by Freemasons. Take these facts with documented proof, Cheikh Anta Diop's work in particular, supporting the ancestral ties of European mason lodges with the Egyptian Mystery Schools as our first clarification for discussion.

Secondly, bring forth the notion that the front of our Great Seal bears a striking resemblance to the African symbol of Horus (the hawk). The Great Seal was designed and adopted by an act of Congress in 1782 (over 5000 years after the creation of the African symbol of Horus). There are indeed a number of similarities. For example, above Horus is the sun, symbolizing power and knowledge. Above the eagle are thirteen stars, known as the constellation, which symbolize the union and strength of thirteen colonies becoming one among the nations of the world. As you can see, both circular symbols represent power and strength. The hawk holds in its talons the "shen," representing infinity. The "ankh," which is seen above the shen, is the African symbol of life. The eagle holds in its left talons thirteen arrows symbolizing war and an olive branch in its right talon with thirteen leaves, representing peace. The eagle's head is looking at the olive branch, indicating peace as the preference of the nation. As you can see, both symbols clearly emphasize life over death. The seal symbolizes the foundations upon which this great nation were built, as does Horus, in part, for Ancient Africa.

Thirdly, enter into the discussion the fact that in Masonic and metaphysical literature, the number *thirteen* represents transformation. Twelve represents the completion of a cycle. Adding one is considered the transformation of the energy of the completed cycle to a higher, more spiritual level. Connect these thoughts with representations for relevance and you see this philosophy symbolized with Jesus Christ and the twelve disciples, the sun and the twelve signs of the zodiac, the mythical King Arthur and his twelve knights of the round table, December 25th and the twelve days of Christmas, and courtroom proceedings which include a judge and twelve members of the jury. For added support of this premise, mention the birthday of the United States, July 4, 1776. After further study, you will find that this date coincided with the astrological sign of Cancer and the number *thirteen* (Ancient Africa was ruled by the sun sign Cancer). What will interest one is the notion that, with this information being considered factual, this country was founded on African principles and built, in part, by African slaves. Continue this focus by considering the fact that July 4, 1776 follows *thirteen* days after the sun entered the sign of Cancer during the summer solstice on June 21, 1776. Look back at the Great Seal. There are *thirteen* leaves and *thirteen* berries on the olive branch, *thirteen* arrows and *thirteen* stripes on the shield, *thirteen* letters in the words "E pluribus unum," *thirteen* stars in the constellation above the eagle's head, and throughout the seal the number *thirteen* is used *thirteen* times. There were *thirteen* colonies at the birth of this country and the *thirteenth* amendment to the constitution freed the slaves.

Continue this train of thought with me. Think of how empowered young African Americans might feel to see their own connection to symbols that previously seemed to exclude them. Again, it's all in the way you look at things.

CASE IN POINT

There was once a young man name Genaria who had a hamster named Mish Mish. Genaria loved his hamster and played with him every day after school. However, at night Genaria could not sleep because Mish Mish would run around in his cage and make all kinds loud, strange and irritating noises. Genaria decided to quiet his hamster down at night by installing an electrical grid on the floor of the cage, all but one section, that is. At night Genaria would cover the cage in darkness and turn on the electrical grid. Each time Mish Mish attempted to move, he received a sharp electrical shock. When the cover was removed and there was light in the cage, there were no electrical shocks, food was readily available, and Genaria would take Mish Mish out of the cage to play. The darkness quickly became associated with hurt and pain. Mish Mish's initial reaction to darkness, blackness, became fright, nervousness, and despair.

This story is delineated to provide a bridge, a connection, bringing relevance to the orientation many African Americans find themselves experiencing today. Our society has created and continues to reinforce stimulus-response situations whereby thoughts and events associated with almost anything black generate fear, anger, caution, and other negative connotations. Other negative connotations include terms such as: Black Magic, Black Cat, Blackmail, Black List, Black Market, Black Monday, and the cowboy wearing the Black Hat. These and other words and symbols are so common in our vocabulary that often it is not the word that is heard, but rather the feelings these words and symbols generate which are critical. Often words and symbols act as subliminal messages.

Now, let us take this issue of black as a skin color or shade and explore subcomponents, used for negative purposes, often in the form of subliminal messages. The issue of shade in relation to the degree of darkness of African Americans has a long history. During slavery, lighter-skinned African Americans, due primarily to the sexual exploits of Anglo slave owners, their sons or overseers, normally performed duties in the house, while all the other slaves were relegated to fieldwork. The lighter skinned slaves, initially due to their mixture of black and white blood, were considered by owners as more intelligent than the pure African. Embodied in the evolution of concepts developed here are the sexual activities instigated by white men and women which resulted in the procreation of the Human Race. However, questions concerning the children these liaisons created took center stage. How should we classify them? Are they black or white, slave or free, mine, yours or ours? Decisions or rulings could prove costly if not well-thought-out. Specifically, certain decisions could greatly diminish some slaveholder's number of slaves and therefore their net worth and potential productivity.

At issue was also one of justification. In order to enslave another human being, a *human being* must develop defense and adjustment mechanisms in order to deal with the situation. They must tell themselves, and find ways to support this form of thinking, that slavery is okay, that these individuals, although they are physically similar, are subhuman rather than fully human like "the rest of us." They create a mind-set that sees the African American as incapable of self-care and self-direction. After much debate, state laws were passed which designated mixed heritage individuals Black and therefore slaves. The states of Virginia and Maryland went so far as to enact legislation that stated that any person with one drop of Black blood would have the same legal status as the African of pure blood. The person was considered Black.

Although many slave owners did not admit to fatherhood in these cases, they still attempted to treat their children with a little more humanity. Often these children of mixed heritage were afforded opportunities unlike those of pure-blood African slaves. Although laws in the South prohibited slaves from learning to read, some were taught in the homes of their masters. Some of these slaves of mixed heritage were even sent North for a more formal education. Light- skinned house slaves suffered less from the grueling labor of the fields. Many took the opportunity of being around their white slave owners to learn the social skills of the white families they served. All, or at least the majority, of slaves benefiting from these opportunities were those of mixed heritage. Mixed-heritage slaves, in many instances, began to see themselves as better than the other slaves. Darker-skinned slaves became envious of the lighter-skinned slaves. Many became angry and even belligerent towards them. These attitudes were lived out within slave quarters, thus creating division between "house niggers" and "field niggers."

Another Way To See Things

These early origins of divisions between light skinned and dark skinned African American slaves continue to be a source of negative imaging. Negative imaging, enhanced by the use of propaganda within a racist society, has proved to be a powerful tool for the enhancement of poor self images among all African Americans. Divisions between the two groups manifest in many ways. Light-skinned Blacks, as a means of securing their perceived status above darker-skinned Blacks, employed, and at times still employ, many of the patterns used by some rich Whites as a way of separating themselves from the masses. Light-skinned Blacks opened exclusive schools for their children, formed business associations among themselves, denying entrance to darker-skinned Blacks. They formed, among other things, their own churches, country clubs and social groups, all with the primary intent to remain separate from the masses of Blacks who were brown and darker in skin color.

Premises discussed in this book state that the current conditions plaguing African Americans stem in part from a high degree of misinformation covert and otherwise. However, if we were to believe in the principle of cause and effect, how would this true information, and other uncovered facts of this type change existing conditions?

> Once you begin to choose the truth of your own reality and begin to build on your own reality as Diop did, as Roberson did, as Elijah did, as Elijah's student—Malcolm X—did, as King did, as Booker T. did—you can begin to use those kinds of concepts to develop a concept that will start to free you. What do all of the African-American men we have discussed have in common? First, they all demanded respect for black women, black family life and working together. They understood that you cannot have liberation by yourself. You have

> to work together within a family network in order to bring about critical change within the society (Akbar, 1991, p. 83).

Well, when one begins to understand the total a new awakening—transformation, an enlightenment will, and has for some, begun to take place. Individuals of this renaissance movement will note its underlying motives and its effects on the psychological, physical and all other aspects of African American life. Social club, business, neighborhood, church and school memberships, to name a few, would no longer be based on criteria such as the *brown bag test* (a test requiring an individual to place his or her arm inside a brown paper bag, resulting in only those with skin lighter than the bag gaining admission). Political, social and educational leadership would be seen in varying shades, instead of our historical preference for mainly the lighter skin being qualified to lead. For example, when looking at pictures of DuBois' "Talented Tenth," one notes that all but one person on the list, Phyllis Wheatley Peters, was light-skinned. When taking a historical look at Black leadership, one notes similar ratios. With this new/old knowledge however, opinions about the intellectual and social capabilities of darker-skinned Blacks would surely change. African Americans determined to change the media coverage weighted negatively toward them would have solid footing to combat these propagated images. Maybe even music videos would describe and present the beauty of the African American woman as it really is. Long silky hair, light skin and narrow nose is not the only representation of beauty. We would realize the propaganda behind this image and begin to recognize beauty as multifaceted perceptions not based on the predetermined attributes decided for the masses, but rather perceptions determined by each individual. Most important, opportunities for success, if not opened by others, would be forced open by those wanting inclusion. In other words, the trickle-down approach to admission into the American social construct would be demolished.

The day to believe and to let the truth be known is here. Now it is up to us, African Americans, to spread the word. We must make this a part of our child development process. I say we, not the schools or other social agencies. After all, despite the good intentions of some, they are all part of a government that has found ways, both in the guise of liberal and conservative reform, to hide or diminish the importance of this knowledge. It is suggested here that we become more visionary in our approach. Reactive measures impede the type of progress necessary. We must become more proactive by seeking pathways that promote the real contributions and truth of the ancestors of us all. This truth will promote realistic, accurate histories all can be proud of and draw strength from. These historical facts help to change experiences, thoughts and then actions of individuals actively working towards desired goals. Due to this paradigm shift, opportunities for success, if not opened by others, will be forced open by those, in mass, wanting inclusion. It is a vehicle for change, the type we seek. Let us do a little revisiting.

SECOND RATE? (REVISITED)

Who are they to determine my walk in this life? Just because some choose to place barriers in my path doesn't mean I can't overcome them. After all, look at what John H. Johnson did. This man moved from Arkansas in 1918 to Chicago with his mother (single parent). At the age of 24 while working as a clerk for the Supreme Liberty Life Insurance Company,

John Johnson began to publish his first magazine called *Negro Digest*. This venture led to his now famous *Ebony* magazine, which has made this African American millions of dollars. Mr. Johnson began as a member of the ranks of the poor, but found a way to traverse the many barriers along his pathway to achieve goals sought. If he can achieve his goals, then so can I. There's nothing second-rate about him, or me. Who do they think they are!

MY PARENTS (REVISITED)

My parents are hard-working, dedicated people. They tell us stories about our ancestors. My father, a strong proud man, says we must have goals. We should begin to think about the type of life we want to live, always placing God first, and then mapping out pathways toward the achievement of desired goals. He says that pathways, the plural form, are very important. My mother, a kind yet stern African American woman, reinforces his comments during our discussions. She says that they will find ways to create barriers never thought about. Being able to choose between moving straight ahead, sideways or even shifting into neutral for a minute or two must be options well-developed in our minds. My parents tell my siblings and me that half the battle is mental. In order to fight from a position of strength, one must become proactive. One must plan ahead and map out possible scenarios of potential situations and be ready to make choices. They say the will to succeed will help as each of us prepares for the future. Regardless of what they might say or do!

LINEAGE (REVISTED)

I know that I have a heritage to be proud of. This has

become a foundation of strength as I face the trials and tribulations of living in this country as an African American. I am very aware of our legacy of scholars, kings, queens and great civilizations. I am proud of the many contributions my ancestors have made to this country and to the world. When they ask me where my father is and just exactly who is my father, I tell them about the oppression that has been placed on the backs of Black America. I also tell them that this is not meant to excuse anything, only to emphasize the fact that those days are days gone by. A new day is upon us which incorporates the great traditions, cultures and contributions of my lineage. Their lineage helps to define who they are; so does mine.

IMPRINTING (REVISITED)

I was only seven, yet I remember the event as if it were today. She was up talking into that microphone, so bold, so beautiful. Her strength was being absorbed by me and remains with me to this day.

Ego Tripping

(there may be a reason why)

i was born in the congo
I walked the fertile crescent and built
the sphinx
I designed a pyramid so tough that a star
    that only glows every one hundred years falls
into the center giving divine perfect light
I am bad

Another Way To See Things

I sat on the throne
drinking nectar with allah
I got hot and sent an ice age to europe
to cool my thirst
My oldest daughter is nefertiti
the tears from my birth pains
created the nile
I am a beautiful woman

I gazed on the forests and burned
out the sahara desert
with a packet of goat's meat
and a change of clothes
I crossed it in two hours
I am a gazelle so swift
so swift you can't catch me

For a birthday present when he was three
I gave my son hannibal an elephant
He gave me rome for mother's day
My strength flows ever on

My son noah built new/ark and
I stood proudly at the helm
as we sailed on a soft summer day
I turned myself into myself and was
jesus
men intone my loving name
All praises All praises
I am the one who would save

I sowed diamonds in my back yard
My bowels deliver uranium
the filings from my fingernails are
semi-precious jewels
On a trip north

Another Way To See Things

I caught a cold and blew
My nose giving oil to the arab world
I am so hip even my errors are correct
I sailed west to reach east and had to round off
        the earth as I went
        The hair from my head thinned and gold was laid
        across three continents

I am so perfect so divine so ethereal so surreal
I cannot be comprehended
        except by my permission

I mean . . .I . . . can fly
        like a bird in the sky

Nikki Giovanni

So I strut a little as I walk. What they say doesn't bother me and they wonder why. Hey, I can do whatever I set my mind to. I mean . . . I . . . can . . . .

LYNCHED (REVISITED)

Lynched, that's what they called it—and they told me just what it meant, too. This group of African Americans were mad, I mean real mad. They said that a man by the name of John Sylvester was stopped by the police in this small town. He was on his way home and took a shortcut that carried him away from the interstate. You see, he had been told his wife was in labor with their first-born while on a business trip. The police said his car was not familiar, so they stopped him. When John seemed a little agitated, because of being stopped and the situation back home, the police thought he might be hiding something, so they took him to the police station. What happened after that not one person seems to know for sure. All we know is that he was found hanging by his necktie in the cell the very next morning. The adults were saying this whole thing sounded fishy and were determined to find the true events of that night and next morning. They said there was only one set of laws for all and that the law would be upheld.

They were right! Less than five months after John's son was born, the three police officers were found guilty of murder and sentenced to death by lethal injection.

JUST ANOTHER KID (REVISITED)

They're just kids and so are we. But their parents won't let them play with us. Their parents call us no-count "niggers" and "shines." They tell their kids, loud enough for us to hear, that they shouldn't play with the cursed of the earth, those half-human darkies. My mother told me to pray for these people. She said that they just needed to seek guidance from the Lord. So I prayed.

Well, they still didn't play with me. But I got over it and later found that they weren't all alike. My wife and I have two children of our own now. We live in a neighborhood with some of them, but now all the kids play together. They have their little spats and disagreements but hey, they're just kids.

BUSING (REVISITED)

Busing began and all the other folk moved out. All the surrounding small towns became cities! Actually, the new businesses moving to the area, with jobs, located in these new cities (the suburbs). The other folk moved, now the jobs are moving too—away from us.

So we decided to seize the opportunity. We formed organizations committed to the improvement of our neighborhoods, schools and community at large. Our organizations made sure the city spent tax money equitably, making sure our parks and schools were well-maintained. We started our own bank, provided small business loans and opened many businesses and therefore jobs. Our people spent their money in the community, thus making repayment of loans easier and new loans possible. Now they want to move some of their businesses back into our community. Our neighborhood revitalization program has helped many of us remodel our homes and provided seed money for the building of new homes.

We have also decreased all forms of crime threefold. So now they want to move back. We've decided to let them.

ANGER (REVISITED)

I am cool, so cool. The police officer pulled me over but I know my rights. I calmly follow his commands, thank him and say good-bye. The last time an officer was offensive and abusive toward me, my tape recorder was playing. So I sent a copy of the tape to the chief and informed him that the next time this happened, copies would be sent to all the news agencies in the county. I always mention the officer's badge number during conversations. This seems to change his approach, for some reason.

THE BERRY (REVISITED)

Is it what they say man—the darker the berry, the sweeter

the juice? Do they really go wild in the hay? I heard your women are the best, in the bed that is.

When I think about African American women, I envision a combination of beauty and strength that is remarkable. I feel warmth, joy, compassion, fortitude, direction. There is an air of possibility, of being aware that you can do, if only you try. Spirituality encircles these and other feelings. A constellation of tremendous magnitude, or greatness.

To tell you the truth, my description is much more accurate, man.

FEELINGS (REVISITED)

We were asked to close our eyes and reflect back to our childhood. .. What I felt, and talked about, was the feelings generated during this reflective process. When thinking about my childhood, before starting school, I get this warm feeling. I know I was loved, cared for. Home, my parents, my family —what a nice place to be. I feel security, trust and a sense that everything is just fine.

We must focus on these feelings in our schools. Schools in which children feel warmth, trust, love, security and success, to name a few attributes. Schools that are productive, proactive environments. These are the types of school needs we must have in place before any real substantive learning will continue to perpetuate itself. I will continue to do my part—what will you do?

THE EYES—LOOK AT HIS EYES (REVISITED)

He came to our class one Monday afternoon. He was dirty,

his clothes were mere rags, and he looked so sad. A group of us decided to become friends with him. We shared our lunch with him and even gave him some of our clothes. Our teacher would take his dirty clothes home and wash them on the weekends. A real surprise came when our principal made him a part-time worker at the school, in the evenings.

I think the one thing that brought back the sparkle in his eyes and the strut in his step was the notion that we liked and cared for the person within, not just the outward presentation. He finally told us this was the first time the word family had any meaning. We were happy.

WE'RE ALL GOD'S CHILDREN (REVISITED)

My parents, and a bunch more, said, "If we are about true integration, then both sides should have an active part in this school district's restructuring." The group of parents were upset with the results of last year's program for school desegregation, its first. Their evaluation demonstrated gross negligence on the part of all adults involved in the project, including themselves. All schools, they said, should be integrated. All schools, they said, should offer a high-quality program designed to provide opportunities for maximum student achievement in both academic and social areas. They wanted the new plan to do away with school-within-a-school segregation practices. The parents also wanted equal access to school facilities, including the library, for all students. They not only presented a plan for the integration of schools, but also for neighborhoods. The plan, the adult part, called initially for a series of awareness-building, get acquainted type gatherings. The other parents, some of them, agreed. Both groups felt getting to know the other was an excellent starting point. We would then get rid of many false impressions of the other. We would see more similarity than difference. We would see that we are all God's Children.

THE POLICE (REVISITED)

The neighborhood police storefront was a very good idea. The program was developed to create more opportunities for positive interaction between the police and community people. But when our principal invited the police into the building as a part of a partnership program, things really got better. Now we know the officers by name and many of them know us. We see them as people and I'm sure the feelings are reciprocal. Anyway, police brutality in our area seems to have disappeared. By the way, the crime rate has also decreased considerably. Things are much nicer, now that we've taken the time to get to know one another.

Finally, I leave you with these thoughts:

BOUNCING BACK

They slapped my face and called me names.
I turned my cheek but it hurt the same,
They said, "Hey Girl! You can't learn that!"
I ignored those lies and I'm bouncing back.

I could not quit, but they had me down.
They faded my dreams and passed me around.
They knew by then that I would crack,
but I fooled them all, I'm bouncing back.

Another Way To See Things

For a while there, I thought I was gone.
Instead of my tune, I was singing their song.
I thought I couldn't learn because I'm Black,
but I changed that tune and I'm bouncing back.

I found a new hope and have a new dream.
Now I know I can do anything.
I know now there is nothing I lack
because I learned how to bounce back.

Yvonne Greene

You see, It Is All In The Way You Look At Things

REFERENCES

—,(1993). Ego Tripping and Other Poems For Young Readers. New York, NY: L. Hill Books.

Adams, Elizabeth L. (1953). Dark Symphony. "Incident," New York, NY: Harper and Brothers.

Akbar, N. (1985). The community of self. Tallahassee, FL: Mind Productions & Associates.

Barnett, B., McQuarrie, F., and Norris, C. (1991). "The Moral Imperatives of Leadership: A Focus On Human Decency." The National Policy Board for Educational Administration, Memphis, TN.

Blaise, J. and Kirby, P.C. (1992). Bringing Out The Best In Teachers: What Effective Principals Do. Newbury Park, CA: Corwin Press.

Brown, Thomas. (March, 1990). "The Impact of Culture on Cognition." The Clearing House, Washington, D.C.

Buffie, E. (1989). The Principal and Leadership. Elementary Principal Series No. 1, Phi Delta Kappa.

Cose, E. (1993). The Rage of a Privileged Class. New York, Harper Collins Pub., Inc.

Cross, R. (1981). What makes an effective principal? Principal, 60(4), 19-22.

Delpit, L. (November, 1986). Skills and Other Dilemmas of a Progressive Black Educator. Harvard Educational Review, 56(4), 379-385.

Delpit, L. (August, 1988). The Silenced Dialogue: Power and Pedagogy in Educating Other People's Children. Harvard Educational Review, 58(3), 280-298.

Ellsworth, E. (1994). Representation, Self-Representation, and the Meanings of Difference: Questions for Educators. In Martusewicz, R. & Reynolds, W. (Eds.). Inside Out: Contemporary Critical Perspectives in Education (pp. 99-108). New York, NY: St. Martin's Press, Inc.

Eubanks, E. & Parish, R. (Summer, 1993). After All the Dinosaurs are Gone: A Cultural Requirement for Restructuring? The NABSE Journal, Vol. 1, No. 2.

Fenstermacher, G. (1990). Some moral considerations on teaching as a profession. In J. Goodlad, R., Soder, K., & Sirotnik (Eds.). The moral dimensions of teaching (pp. 130-151). San Francisco, CA: Jossey-Bass Publishers.

Fordham, S., & Ogbu, J. (1986). Black students' school success: Coping with the burden of "acting White". Urban Review, 18(3), 1-31.

Francis-Okongwu, A. & Pflaum, S. (1993). Diversity in Education: Implications for Teacher Preparation. In Celebrating Diverse Voices. Newbury Park, CA: Corwin Press, Inc. pp. 112-132.

Gibson, M. (1988). Accommodation without assimilation: Sikh immigrants in an American high school and community. Ithaca, NY: Cornell University Press.

Giovanni, N. (1994). Racism 101. New York: William Morrow and Company, Inc.

Glickman, C. (1990). Supervision of Instruction: A Developmental Approach. Boston, Allyn and Bacon.

Goldman, L. (1992). The Misconception Of Culture And The Perversion Of Multiculturalism. Proceedings: Southwestern Philosophy of Education Society, Vol. XLII.

Goodlad, John. (1990). Teachers For Our Nation's Schools. Jossey-Bass Publishers, San Francisco, CA.

Haberman, M. The Pedagogy of Poverty Versus Good Teaching. Phi Delta Kappan, 73, 4 (December, 1991), 290-294.

Hamilton, P. (1990). Strategies For A New African American Renaissance: Fusing African World Culture + H.O.T.S. + Excellence. Paper presented at the 18th Annual Conference for the National Alliance of Black School Educators, November, 1990.

Hill, P., Wuchitech, J., & Williams, R. (February, 1980). The effects of federal education program on school principals. A Rand Note Prepared for the U.S. Department of Health, Education and Welfare. Santa Monica: The Rand Corporation.

Hodgkinson, H. (April, 1993). "American Education: The Good, the Bad, And the Task." Kappan, Vol. 74, No. 8.

Holmes Group. (1990). "Tomorrow's Schools: Principles For The Design Of Professional Development Schools." The Holmes Group, Inc. East Lansing, MI.

Jencks, C. (1972). Inequality. New York: Harper & Row.

Kierstead, F. (1992). Ethnical considerations of Multicultural Education In American Public Schools. Proceedings: Southwestern Philosophy of Education Society, Vol. XLII.

Kirstol, I. In Van Patten, J., Bolding, J., & Reilly, R. (September, 1992). Fragmentation In American Society: Impact On Education. Proceedings: Southwestern Philosophy Of Education Society.

Lincoln, C. (1993). "The DuBoisian dubiety and the American Dilemma." In Early, G. (Ed.). Lure and Loathing (pp. 19). New York, NY: Penguin Press.

Loden, M., & Rosener, J. (1991). Workforce America? Managing employee diversity as a vital resource. Homewood, IL: Business One Irwin Publishers.

Loury, G. (1993). "Free at Last? A Personal Perspective on Race and Identity in America." In Early, G. (Ed.). Lure and Loathing (pp. 1-12). New York, NY: Penguin Press.

McLean, Vianne. (Winter, 1990). "Early Childhood Teachers in Multicultural Settings." The Educational Forum, Columbus, OH.

Morgan, D. (1986). Images of Organizations. Cambridge, MA: Sage Publications.

Murphey, D. (June, 1991). Multiculturalism: Its Implications for A Free Society. Conservative Review, 2.

Nelson-LeGall, S., & Jones, E. (November, 1991). Classroom Help-Seeking behavior Of African-American Children. Education And Urban Society, Vol. 24, No. 1.

Nieto, S. and Sinclair, R. (1991). Leadership and the Expanded Environment for Learning. In Barnett, B., McQuarrie, F., and Norris, C. (Eds). The Moral Imperatives of Leadership: A Focus on Human Decency. Memphis, TN: National Network for Innovative Principal Preparation.

Nobles, W. (1986). African Psychology: Toward Its Reclamation, Reassertion, and Revitalization. Oakland: Black Family Institute.

Norris, C. (1994). Cultivating Creative Cultures. In Huges (Eds.) The Principal As Leader, 61-87. New York: Maacmillan.

Ogbu, J. (Autumn, 1992). Adaptation to Minority Status and Impact on School Success. Theory Into Practice, 31(4), 287-295.

Parham, T. (1993). Psychological Storms: The African American Struggle for Identity. Chicago, IL: African American Images.

Peterson, K.D. (1982). Making sense of principal's work. The Australian Administrator, 3(3).

Prothrow-Stith, D. (1991). Deadly Consequences. New York, NY: HarperCollins Publishers.

Robinson, G. (May, 1988). Some popular assertions about school administration: Are they myths or realities? Concerns in Education, Educational Research Service.

Sergiovanni, T. (1990). Value-added Leadership: How To Get Extraordinary Performance In Schools. New York: Harcourt Brace Jovanovich.

Simpson, D. (1959). "Cassell's New Latin Dictionary." New York: Funk & Wagnalls.

Smith, S. & Borgstedt, K. (1985). Factors Influencing Adjustment of White Faculty in Predominantly Black Colleges. Journal of Negro Education, Vol. 54, No. 2.

Taylor, A. (November,1991). Social Competence and The Early School Transition: Risk and Protective Factors for African-American Children. Education And Urban Society, Vol. 24, No.1.

Taylor, Susan L. (September, 1994). "In The Spirit". Essence.

Thomas, A. and Sillen, S. (1972). Racism and Psychiatry. New York, NY. Citadel Press.

Thomas, C. (1990). A DELPHI STUDY: Developing a model for improving the process of evaluating the school principal. Doctoral Dissertation. East Texas State University, Commerce, TX.

Thomas, C. (February, 1992). Inviting Students To Learn. NABSE Journal.

Thomas, C. & Simpson, D. (In Press). Community and Collegiality in Diverse Settings: A Conflict of Interest in the Professorate? Journal of Negro Education.

Thomas, C. and Vornberg, J. (December, 1991). Evaluation Prinpals: New Requirements, Directions for the '90s. NASSP Bulletin.

Tyler, R. (1991). The Moral Imperative of Educational Leadership. In Barnett, B., McQuarrie, F., and Norris, C. (Eds). The Moral Imperatives of Leadership: A Focus on Human Decency. Memphis, TN: National Network for Innovative Principal Preparation.

Varney, S. and Crusher, K. (October, 1990.) Understanding Cultural Diversity Can Improve Intercultural Interactions. NASSP Bulletin.

West, C. (1993). Race Matters. Boston, Beacon Press.

Wilson, W. (1985). Cycles of deprivation and the underclass debate. Social Service Review, 59, 541-559.

Wynn, M. (1992). Empowering African American Males To Succeed, S. Pasadena, CA: Rising Sun Publishing.

INDEX